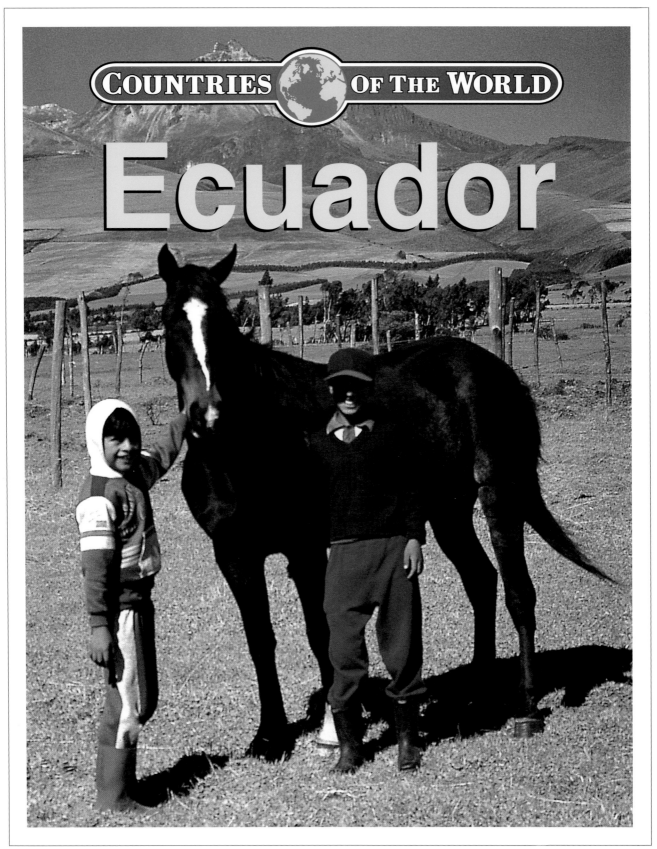

COUNTRIES OF THE WORLD

Ecuador

Gareth Stevens Publishing
A WORLD ALMANAC EDUCATION GROUP COMPANY

About the Author: Amy S. Daniels is a graduate of Brigham Young University. She spent two years in Ecuador doing volunteer work, which gave her the opportunity to gain valuable insight into Ecuadorian culture. Daniels has written on a freelance basis for various academic publications.

PICTURE CREDITS
Andes Press Agency: 19, 22
Michele Burgess: 1, 3 (bottom), 9, 23, 36,
     45, 48, 89
Jan Butchofsky-Houser: 71, 74
Camera Press Ltd.: 83
Consulate of Ecuador: 15 (top), 15 (center)
Victor Englebert: 3 (center), 6 (both), 25, 29,
     35, 39, 40, 61, 68, 73
Roberto Falck: 64, 72
Eduardo Gil: 26, 65
Hulton Getty/ Archive Photos: 15 (bottom),
     16, 50, 51, 53, 62, 75, 76, 77, 79, 80,
     81, 82
The Hutchison Library: 7 (top), 20, 33
Björn Klingwall: 14, 60, 84
Jason Lauré: 4
JHU/CCP: 78
North Wind Pictures: 11, 59
Chip and Rosa María Peterson: 5, 12, 17,
     21, 24, 27, 28, 30, 32, 34, 38, 46, 47, 49
Pietro Scozzari: cover, 41, 43
South American Pictures: 3 (top), 8, 13, 18,
     37, 42, 44, 52, 54, 66, 67, 85, 87, 91
Tan Chung Lee: 10, 69
Times Editions: 90 (both)
Topham Picturepoint: 2, 56, 63, 70
Trip Photographic Library: 7 (bottom), 31,
     55, 57 (both), 58

Digital Scanning by Superskill Graphics Pte Ltd

Written by
AMY S. DANIELS

Edited by
YUMI NG

Edited in the U.S. by
**PATRICIA LANTIER
MONICA RAUSCH**

Designed by
JAILANI BASARI

Picture research by
SUSAN JANE MANUEL

First published in North America in 2002 by
Gareth Stevens Publishing
A World Almanac Education Group Company
330 West Olive Street, Suite 100
Milwaukee, Wisconsin 53212 USA

Please visit our web site at
www.garethstevens.com
For a free color catalog describing
Gareth Stevens' list of high-quality books
and multimedia programs, call
1-800-542-2595 (USA) or
1-800-461-9120 (CANADA).
Gareth Stevens Publishing's
Fax: (414) 332-3567.

© **TIMES MEDIA PRIVATE LIMITED 2002**
Originated and designed by
Times Editions
An imprint of Times Media Private Limited
A member of the Times Publishing Group
Times Centre, 1 New Industrial Road
Singapore 536196
http://www.timesone.com.sg/te

Library of Congress Cataloging-in-Publication Data
Daniels, Amy S.
Ecuador / by Amy S. Daniels.
p. cm. — (Countries of the world)
Includes bibliographical references and index.
Summary: An introduction to the geography, history, government, lifestyles, culture, and current issues of the South American country of Ecuador.
ISBN 0-8368-2343-5 (lib. bdg.)
1. Ecuador—Juvenile literature. [1. Ecuador.] I. Title.
II. Countries of the world (Milwaukee, Wis.)
F3708.5.D36   2002
986.6—dc21   2001042836

Printed in Malaysia

1 2 3 4 5 6 7 8 9 06 05 04 03 02

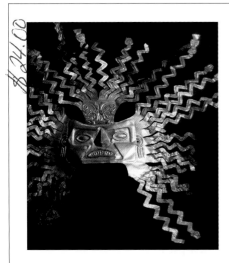

Contents

AN OVERVIEW OF ECUADOR

One of the smallest countries in South America, Ecuador takes its name from the equator, which crosses the country just north of Quito, the capital city. Although small in size, Ecuador has remarkable geographic and cultural diversity. Native Indian peoples still inhabit many areas of the country, where they have kept their traditional cultures while adapting their lifestyles to the pace of modern society. Many Ecuadorians live and work in the bustling cities of Quito and Guayaquil, where the mix of modern and colonial architecture reflects Ecuador's rich past and vibrant future. With its majestic volcanoes, sparkling shores, rain forests, and Galápagos Islands, Ecuador is a land of endless discovery.

Opposite: **Ecuadorian children gather at** *La Mitad del Mundo* **(lah mee-TAHD dehl MOON-doh) monument, which marks the site of the equator north of Quito.**

Below: **Ecuadorians are warm and friendly people. These students from Ambato smile readily for the camera.**

THE FLAG OF ECUADOR

The Ecuadorian flag consists of three horizontal stripes that are yellow, blue, and red. The yellow stripe is twice as wide as the blue and red stripes. Yellow symbolizes the abundance and fertility of the crops and land. Blue signifies the color of the sea and sky. Red represents the blood shed by soldiers in the battles for independence. The coat of arms lies at the center of the flag. The condor at the top protects the country under its outstretched wings, but it also stands ready to attack any enemy. Ecuador's highest mountain, Chimborazo, and the steamboat *Guayas* are located in the center of the coat of arms.

Geography

Ecuador's total area of 109,483 square miles (283,560 square kilometers) includes the country's territory on the South American continent as well as the Galápagos Islands. The country is about the size of the U.S. state of Colorado. Ecuador is bordered by Colombia to the north, Peru to the east and south, and the Pacific Ocean to the west. Despite its size, Ecuador is one of the most geographically diverse countries in the world. This small country has four distinct regions: the Coastal Lowland; the Andes Highlands; the Eastern Lowland, or Amazon Region; and the Galápagos Islands.

Above: The Amazon Jungle in Ecuador is home to the largest variety of wildlife in the world.

The Regions

The Coastal Lowland, or *Costa* (KOHS-tah), is a flat plain about 100 miles (160 km) wide that extends along the Pacific coast of Ecuador. Rivers that begin high in the Andes Mountains carry mud and debris from the mountains down to the coastline. The different types of soil deposited by the rivers make the ground of the lowlands fertile for agriculture but unstable for construction. The Costa's main rivers are the Esmeraldas and the Guayas.

Below: The spectacular shores of Salinas beach along Ecuador's Pacific coast are a popular holiday spot for locals and tourists.

The Andes Highlands, or *Sierra* (see-EH-rah), takes its name from the Andes Mountains, which extend the length of Ecuador from north to south. These mountains can be over 20,000 feet (6,096 meters) high, and many of the mountains are active volcanoes. In fact, Ecuador is home to the highest active volcano in the world, Cotopaxi, at 19,348 feet (5,897 m).

The Eastern Lowland, or *Oriente* (oh-ree-EHN-teh), is the largest geographical region of Ecuador and consists mainly of the Amazon Jungle. Consequently, this region is also known as the Amazon Region, and it is mostly made up of uninhabited tropical rain forests. These forests extend from the eastern foothills of the Andes to the Amazon River Basin. Numerous rivers flow through this region, including the Napo and Pastaza.

The Galápagos Islands are located about 600 miles (965 km) off the coast of Ecuador in the Pacific Ocean. Known in Spanish as the *Archipiélago de Colón* (ahr-chee-pee-EH-lah-goh deh koh-LONE), these islands have a land area of 3,093 square miles (8,010 square km). Most of the mountain peaks on the Galápagos are volcanoes.

Above: **The impressive Chimborazo Volcano in the Andes is Ecuador's highest peak at 20,561 feet (6,267 m).**

Below: **Rare species of plants, such as the tall variety of the prickly pear cactus, thrive on the Galápagos Islands.**

THE AMAZON JUNGLE

The largest rain forest in the world, the Amazon Jungle is filled with a wide variety of plants and animals. Many native peoples also live in the jungle. The Ecuadorian government has set up laws to protect these native peoples and their environment.
(A Closer Look, page 44)

Left: **Myriad varieties of beautiful orchids flourish in the wild in Ecuador's Amazon rain forest.**

Climate

The climate in Ecuador is extremely variable. Although the country's location near the equator makes most of Ecuador a tropical country, temperatures vary according to altitude. The Sierra has a moderate climate all year round, with temperatures averaging 60° Fahrenheit (15° Celsius). At higher altitudes, however, the climate in the Sierra is much colder, with snow and frost covering the ground most of the year. The Eastern Lowland is hot and humid all year long. The Coastal Lowland is mostly hot and humid as well. Ocean currents, however, make the climate in the Costa cooler than in the Amazon Jungle.

Seasons

Seasons in Ecuador are generally divided into a rainy season and a dry season. On average, the rainy season begins in January and ends in May. The dry season, considered the most enjoyable time of year, lasts from June through December.

Plants and Animals

Ecuador has one of the most diverse ecosystems of plants and animals on Earth. The country's varied regions provide homes for a large variety of plant and animal species.

THE GIANT TORTOISE

The giant tortoise of the Galápagos Islands lives longer than any other creature on Earth. This tortoise species was in danger of becoming extinct due to uncontrolled hunting, but it is now protected by a research and rescue station located on the Galápagos Islands.
(A Closer Look, page 58)

Ecuador has more plant species than Europe, which is nearly thirty times larger than Ecuador. More than eighteen thousand plant species grow in Ecuador, of which about four thousand are endemic, or found only in Ecuador. The northern coast and the Eastern Lowland are covered with tropical jungle. Valuable balsa trees, which are used for lumber, and rubber trees have nearly disappeared from the coast due to large-scale exploitation. Certain species of orchids are also close to extinction. Many plants in the Amazon Region have medicinal purposes. The cinchona tree is the main source of quinine, a medicine used to treat malaria.

Ecuador is home to over 300 species of mammals and more than 1,500 bird species. All reptile species found in the world, as well as an outstanding number of exotic freshwater fish, such as the piranha and the stingray, are native to Ecuador's Amazon Jungle. The Andes Mountains are home to the llama; the alpaca, an animal similar to the llama; and the mountain tapir, which is a black, woolly animal. The Andean condor flies high over Ecuador's mountains. Unusual animals, such as the blue-footed booby and the giant tortoise, along with many plant species, live on the Galápagos Islands.

GALÁPAGOS ISLANDS

The Galápagos Islands are home to rare species of plants and animals. English naturalist Charles Darwin made many of the observations that formed the basis for his ideas on evolution while visiting the Galápagos in 1835.
(A Closer Look, page 56)

Left: **The llama is native to the Andes Mountains. Many Ecuadorians use llamas as a means of transportation and as a source of meat and wool.**

History

Early History

Remains of ancient civilizations dating back thousands of years indicate that Ecuador's earliest inhabitants were hunters and gatherers. By 3000 B.C., distinct civilizations had emerged, which left behind fine examples of pottery, metal objects, and other artifacts. Most of these early civilizations, such as the Valdivia, La Tolita, and Manta cultures, flourished along the Pacific coast. Eventually, these early inhabitants were conquered by the powerful Inca Empire of Peru in the late 1400s.

Incan Rule

The Incan leaders unified the early Ecuadorians by teaching them the Quechua language. In 1532, a civil war broke out between the two sons of the Inca Huayna Capac. Prince Huascar, the legitimate heir, and Prince Atahualpa, a younger son by an Ecuadorian princess, fought for the Incan throne. Atahualpa defeated Huascar in a battle near Riobamba, but the civil war divided and weakened the empire considerably.

PREHISTORY

Many metal objects and ancient pieces of pottery have been found in Ecuador. Experts believe these artifacts are remains of one of the oldest civilizations on the American continents.

(A Closer Look, page 66)

Below: **The temple of Inga Pirca in Cañar Province was built by the Incas.**

The Spanish Conquest

At around this time, Spanish conquistador Francisco Pizarro and his army arrived in Peru in search of gold. Pizarro attacked and conquered the Inca Empire with only two hundred men. Pizarro held Atahualpa for ransom, which the Incas duly paid, but Pizarro eventually executed him. In 1534, Rumiñahui, an Ecuadorian general under Atahualpa, burned the city of Quito to keep the Spaniards from taking it. In spite of Rumiñahui's efforts, Quito was captured and rebuilt by the Spaniards.

Under Spanish rule, natives were forced to work the agricultural fields of the Spanish *encomiendas* (ehn-koh-mee-EHN-dahs). Through the system of encomiendas, the colonial government granted Spanish settlers a piece of land along with its natural resources and Indian population. In return, the Spanish settlers had to defend the land in the event of attacks. They were also responsible for converting the Indian population to Christianity and for extracting the annual tax paid to the Spanish king in gold and local produce. Due to its lack of mineral resources, Ecuador remained a rural colony throughout the Spanish colonial period. Some native Indians were forced to work in textile shops. The Spaniards also imported African slaves to work on the plantations along the coast.

Above: This print shows the scene of the first meeting between the Inca Atahualpa and Spanish conquistador Francisco Pizarro. Atahualpa was later imprisoned and accused of heresy by the Spaniards for rejecting the Bible that was handed to him during this meeting.

Independence from Spain

In the early 1800s, French forces led by Napoleon Bonaparte invaded Spain and placed Joseph, Napoleon's brother, on the Spanish throne. This move led to a series of revolts both in Spain and in the colonies against the new king. In Ecuador, Spanish settlers formed a revolt against the new colonial representative sent by the French emperor. Amid this time of political instability for Spain, the *criollos* (kree-OH-yohs), people of pure Spanish descent born in the Spanish colonies, began to voice their discontent at the unfairness of the colonial political system. This system granted power and privileges only to the *peninsulares* (pay-neen-soo-LAH-rehs), or Spaniards born in Spain.

The climate of political unrest eventually culminated in the fight for independence from Spain by the Latin American colonies. This fight was led by Venezuelan Simón Bolívar and Argentinian José de San Martín. General Antonio José de Sucre, a commander under Bolívar, defeated the Spaniards in the Battle of Pichincha on May 24, 1822, ending the Spanish rule of Ecuador. In the same year, Ecuador joined the confederation of La Gran Colombia. Organized by Simón Bolívar, the confederation consisted of Colombia, Ecuador, and Venezuela. In 1830, the confederation was dissolved, and the three countries became independent nations. Ecuador then took its name from the equator, which runs north of Quito, the country's capital city.

QUITO

The capital of Ecuador, Quito, takes its name from the Quitu, an ancient civilization that inhabited the area prior to the Incan conquest. Today, the city of Quito is divided into two sections — the Old City and the New City.
(A Closer Look, page 68)

Left: A mural in Quito displays the portrait of Simón Bolívar, the Venezuelan who led the fight for independence from Spain in many South American countries.

Left: An Ecuadorian Indian from Azuay Province in the early 1940s cuts stones to be used as pavement. Independence from Spain did not improve living conditions for native Ecuadorian Indians, whose needs remained overlooked by the governments of the young republic.

The Young Republic

Independence from Spain did not change the lives of the native Indians, who had been subjected to years of slavery by the Spanish conquerors. The indigenous peoples' social conditions were ignored by the criollo ruling groups, which were more concerned with staying in power than seeing to the needs of the Indians. A great rivalry between the criollo elite of Quito, the conservative capital in the highlands, and Guayaquil, the main coastal seaport, kept the country from attaining political unity.

Gabriel García Moreno, who enjoyed the support of the Roman Catholic Church, became president of Ecuador in 1861. García Moreno made great efforts to bring progress to Ecuador by planning and overseeing the construction of roads, railroads, schools, and hospitals. Agricultural production, industry, and international trade also rose considerably during his presidency. Like other presidents before him, however, García Moreno was a dictator. He was assassinated in 1875.

General José Eloy Alfaro Delgado, a member of the Liberal Party, took control of the Ecuadorian government in 1895. Alfaro Delgado, who had the support of businessmen from Guayaquil, ended the links between the government and the Roman Catholic Church. Although he did much to modernize Ecuador, the native population remained overlooked and exploited.

GUAYAQUIL

The largest city in Ecuador, Guayaquil is a bustling center of commerce and the country's main seaport. Guayaquil has a long history — the port was one of the first cities founded by the Spaniards in Ecuador.

(*A Closer Look,* page 60)

Left: José María Velasco Ibarra (*right*) was a charismatic and astute politician who used his powerful gift of rhetoric to inspire the masses and attack his political opponents.

Modern History

In 1941, a border dispute arose between Ecuador and Peru. Peru had invaded territory in the Amazon Basin that was previously claimed by Ecuador. War followed, and Peru was eventually given the land in a settlement, the Rio Protocol, signed in 1942 by leaders of Ecuador, Peru, Argentina, Brazil, Chile, and the United States.

In 1948, Galo Plaza Lasso, the leader of a coalition of liberals and socialists, was elected president and served a four-year term. José María Velasco Ibarra, who had served as president twice before, became president again by popular vote in 1952. Velasco Ibarra served as president for a total of five times, from 1934 to 1935, 1944 to 1947, 1952 to 1956, 1960 to 1961, and 1968 to 1972.

In 1997, President Abdalá Bucaram Ortíz was removed from office by the Ecuadorian legislature. Jamil Mahuad was elected president the following year. Although Mahuad was able to finalize a satisfactory peace treaty with Peru over the border dispute, which the Rio Protocol had failed to resolve, financial problems in Ecuador led to dissatisfaction with his presidency. On January 21, 2000, Mahuad fled the presidential palace during demonstrations. The next day, Mahuad stepped down and declared Gustavo Noboa, the vice president, his successor. Noboa's term in office is scheduled to end in January 2003.

ECUADOR–PERU BORDER CONFLICT

The biggest diplomatic issue in Ecuador's history was a long dispute with Peru over territory along the country's southern border. The conflict was finally resolved in 1998.

(*A Closer Look, page 52*)

José Eloy Alfaro Delgado (1842–1912)

The leader of the Radical Liberal Party in Ecuador, José Eloy Alfaro Delgado became president of Ecuador in 1895 and again in 1906. Alfaro's government dismantled the administrative structure set up during the previous conservative era, focusing strongly on separating the Catholic Church from Ecuador's government. Alfaro, however, is mostly remembered for completing the Quito–Guayaquil railroad that was started by his conservative predecessor, President García Moreno. Alfaro tried to improve the conditions of the poor. During his rule, the unfair system of peonage, which had plunged the natives into an endless cycle of debt, was regulated by the government. Alfaro was killed by supporters of the military government in 1912.

José Eloy Alfaro Delgado

Galo Plaza Lasso (1906–1987)

Galo Plaza Lasso was the son of former Ecuadorian president Leónidas Plaza Gutiérrez. Plaza was born and educated in the United States. He served as Ecuador's ambassador to the United States and signed the Charter of the United Nations before becoming president of Ecuador in 1948. Plaza was an advocate of democratic government. During his presidency, he guaranteed freedom of the press and freedom for individuals to voice their opinions, even if these opinions were against the government. Plaza also encouraged the production and export of bananas to the United States, which led to Ecuador's banana boom and relative economic stability. Plaza was secretary general of the Organization of American States from 1968 to 1975.

Galo Plaza Lasso

Rosalía Arteaga Serrano (1956–)

Rosalía Arteaga Serrano, a lawyer by training, became Ecuador's first woman vice president when she joined Abdalá Bucaram Ortíz as his presidential running mate in 1996. Arteaga was president of Ecuador for three days after Bucaram was removed from office by the country's legislature in February 1997. Ecuador's legislature eventually elected Fabián Alarcón president, with Arteaga as his vice president.

Rosalía Arteaga Serrano

15

Government and the Economy

Branches of Government

Ecuador is a republic with a government elected democratically by the people. A president is elected to a four-year term. The president is both the chief of state and the head of government. He or she may not serve two consecutive terms, according to the Constitution of 1998. The president is a member of the executive branch of government along with fourteen Cabinet members. The legislative body of government is represented by the National Congress made up of 121 elected members. Congress meets only two months each year, unless a special session is called. Among judicial government bodies, the Supreme Court is the highest court in the nation. Supreme Court justices are chosen by Congress and are appointed for life. The Supreme Court chooses members for the Superior Court, and the Superior Court appoints civil and penal judges.

SAVING THE ENVIRONMENT

Ecuador has one of the richest ecosystems on Earth. The Ecuadorian government and other private organizations are working hard to preserve the environment for future generations.
(A Closer Look, page 70)

Left: Ecuadorian president Gustavo Noboa and his wife, María Isabel Baquerizo, greet the crowds from the government palace in Quito. Noboa became president of Ecuador on January 22, 2000. He replaced President Jamil Mahuad, who was forced to resign by the National Congress.

Ecuador has twenty-two provinces, or states. Each province has a governor selected by the president, except for Galápagos, which is administered by the Ministry of National Defense. Each province is divided into cantons, or municipalities, and each canton is divided into parishes. The president or the executive branch of government appoints each political chief of the cantons and each political lieutenant of the parishes. Residents elect municipal, or city, mayors by direct vote.

Political Parties

Ecuador has numerous political parties. Since no political party is popular throughout the entire country, these parties often form alliances in order to win elections. Many political leaders organize their own political party when they run for office. Some of the more popular political parties among the people are the Roldosista, the Popular Democracy, the Social Christian Party, the Democratic Leftist Party, the Concentration of Popular Forces, and the Ecuadorian Conservative Party.

Economy

Ecuador's economy is divided into three major areas: agriculture, manufacturing, and services. Ecuador's main export is petroleum, with bananas, cocoa, coffee, and shrimp as other important exports. Since Ecuador's economy relies heavily on the export of raw materials to countries abroad, variations in world market prices significantly affect Ecuador's economy. The United States is Ecuador's most important trading partner. Other countries that also trade with Ecuador include Colombia, Italy, and Japan. Ecuador imports mostly vehicles, chemicals, and machinery.

Agriculture

Most of the country's workforce is employed in the agricultural sector. Throughout the Costa, plantations grow bananas, cacao, coffee, sugar, oranges, and rice. Most of these products are grown for export. In the Sierra, the main crops are potatoes and corn, which are grown for home consumption. Farming techniques remain primitive, although volunteer and university groups have started teaching modern farming methods to farmers.

Below: Ecuador is one of the largest producers and exporters of bananas in the world. Ecuador exports most of its bananas to the United States.

Left: **Fishing provides a livelihood for many Ecuadorian families along the Pacific coast. The government of Ecuador has strict rules about allowing foreign vessels to fish in waters located near the country's coastline.**

Industry

The mining and manufacturing industries greatly increased after oil was discovered in Ecuador in the 1970s. Ecuador is the fourth largest oil exporter in Latin America. Petroleum exports account for about 50 percent of government revenue. In recent years, due to free trade agreements with Colombia and Venezuela, Ecuador has expanded its manufacturing industry, and the export of manufactured products to these two countries has increased. Most of the products, such as pharmaceutical products and textiles, come from Guayaquil and Quito.

The Workforce

Ecuador has a workforce of about 4.2 million people. The workforce is divided mostly by race, or ethnic heritage. Ecuadorians of European descent work as merchants, bankers, or industrialists. Many of them also own large plantations on the coast or in the highlands. *Mestizos* (mehs-TEE-sohs), or people of mixed European and Indian descent; native Indians; and Afro-Ecuadorians make up much of the manual labor workforce. Ecuador has an unemployment rate of about 12 percent.

DOLLARIZATION

Ecuador's severe economic crisis in the 1990s led to an extreme economic measure. The Ecuadorian government adopted the U.S. dollar as the country's official currency in 1999.

(A Closer Look, page 50)

People and Lifestyle

A Mix of Peoples

The population in Ecuador consists of unique groups of people. Descendants of the Spanish settlers as well as other European immigrants make up only 10 percent of the total population of about 12.9 million people. The majority of the population, about 55 percent, consists of mestizos. Indigenous Indians account for 25 percent of the population. About 9 percent of the population is of African descent. Ecuador also has a small Chinese minority.

Below: **An Ecuadorian family in Esmeraldas relaxes on the porch of its home. People living in the Esmeraldas Province are mainly Ecuadorians of African descent.**

Social Classes

Ecuadorians of European descent are the elite social class in Ecuador. These Ecuadorians live in the nation's big cities, such as Quito and Guayaquil. Their lifestyle is heavily influenced by European customs and traditions.

Mestizos, native Indians, and Ecuadorians of African descent mostly work as construction workers, agricultural laborers, or as fishermen on the coast. These groups must work hard for their living, and some of these Ecuadorians have two or three different jobs.

The economic and social divide between Ecuadorians is extreme. People are either poor or wealthy. Naturally, exceptions among the social classes can be found. Some Indians, mestizos, and Afro-Ecuadorians have managed to become merchants, landowners, or professionals in fields, such as education and medicine.

The government is trying to close the gap between the social classes in Ecuador by setting up literacy programs to enable the poorer Quechua-speaking Indians to learn Spanish.

Family Life

Both Spanish and Indian traditions place great emphasis on the family. Extended family life is common in Ecuador. Families care for aging grandparents at home and often open their homes to newlywed children who cannot afford to buy or rent accommodations on their own. Grandparents, parents, children, and even great-grandchildren live in the same house, sometimes for their entire lives.

Above: **Four men enjoy a game of cards outdoors. Traditionally, Ecuadorian men spend much of their spare time visiting friends.**

Gender Roles in the Family

In the typical Ecuadorian household, the father is the wage earner, and the mother takes care of the family. Traditionally, the father, as the head of the family, spends his leisure time as he pleases. Most Ecuadorian men enjoy eating, drinking, or chatting with friends at the local bar or coffee shop. On the other hand, women are responsible not only for all matters within the home, but they also try to make extra money by working as shopkeepers or by selling crops or crafts at local markets. These traditional roles are slowly changing.

Compadrazgo

The system of *compadrazgo* (kohm-pah-DRAHZ-goh), or godparenting, is an inherent part of Ecuadorian culture. This practice stems from Roman Catholic tradition. When a child is born, his or her parents choose a set of godparents for the child's baptism. The godparent usually has no genetic ties to the family, though there are some exceptions, and is a good friend of the parents. Godparents take their role seriously; they take part in the upbringing and the general welfare of the child.

Above: **An Otavalan couple, dressed in traditional wedding attire, leaves the church after the wedding ceremony.**

CUENCA

The city of Cuenca was founded by the Spaniards in 1557. Since then, Cuenca has flourished as a center for beautiful arts and handicrafts, including the world-famous Panama hats.

(A Closer Look, page 48)

Quinceañera

A rite of passage for a young woman in Ecuador is the celebration of her fifteenth birthday, known as *quinceañera* (keen-seh-ah-nee-EH-rah). One of the most anticipated events in a girl's life, preparations for the party may begin months before the actual day. The young woman wears a dress that resembles a wedding dress. She dances the first waltz with her father, thereafter taking turns with the male attendees of the party. The quinceañera celebration is similar to a wedding celebration.

Family Vacations

Ecuadorian families plan their vacations according to their children's summer holidays from school. Families living on the coast take vacations during the months of February and March. Families in the highlands take vacations during the months of July and August. This difference in timing is due to the remarkable contrast in climate between the two regions. Many affluent families spend their vacations at beach resorts.

FAMOUS SITES

From the beautiful landscapes along the Avenue of Volcanoes to its charming colonial towns to the exact site of "half of the world," Ecuador offers many attractions to visitors and locals.

(*A Closer Look, page 54*)

Below: Urban Ecuadorian families like to spend time outdoors at the many beautiful city parks.

Education

All children are required by law to attend elementary school and three years of secondary school, both of which are provided free to all Ecuadorian citizens. Elementary and secondary schools each offer six-year programs. Almost all schools require uniforms, and students must buy their own books and supplies. Most of the schools are located in the bigger cities, so children in rural areas have less opportunities to attend school. The literacy rate in Ecuador is about 90 percent. Most Ecuadorians above fifteen years of age are able to read and write, although the number of literate adults in rural areas is much lower than in the cities.

Below: **Students wearing typical school uniforms wait to board a school bus in the province of Cañar.**

Universities and Libraries

Ecuador has twelve state universities, five private universities, and ten technical, or vocational, schools. The Pontifical Catholic University in Quito is one of the most prestigious universities in Ecuador. Education is a high priority for Ecuadorians. Parents encourage their children to pursue higher education, although many students cannot afford the high costs.

Ecuador's many libraries offer extensive collections of books on a variety of subjects. The Ecuadorian Library Aurelio Espinosa Pólit, located in Quito, is the country's main library. Other major libraries are located within the country's largest universities.

Jurar la Bandera

All Ecuadorian elementary and secondary schools hold a formal patriotic ceremony once a year. *Jurar la Bandera* (who-RAHR lah bahn-DEH-rah), or Allegiance to the Flag, is a ceremony in which each student marches up to the flagpole and pledges allegiance to the flag of Ecuador. Families and friends of the students gather in the school's courtyard to witness this traditional ceremony. School parades are also popular and are normally held on patriotic holidays. Students march on the streets in almost military fashion. The top student of the school marches in front carrying the nation's flag.

Literacy Programs

The Ecuadorian government has set up literacy programs around the country, especially in the rural areas, to give children and adults the opportunity to learn how to read and write in Spanish. The greatest difficulty with this program, however, is the lack of time students have for learning. In the poorer areas, all family members, including the youngest children, must work for a living. If anyone in the family stops work to attend school, the family may not make enough money to buy food or clothing. A lack of professional teachers is another problem in these programs, since most trained teachers work in the cities.

Above: **Quechua-speaking children attend class at a rural school in the province of Napo.**

Religion

Since the Spanish conquest, the Roman Catholic Church has been a major influence in the life and culture of the Ecuadorian people. The church was the first organization to begin a system of formal education for the people. Charity organizations also began with the Catholic Church. The Constitution of 1945 declared freedom of religion and the separation of church and state. From the 1960s to the 1980s, Catholic bishops became increasingly involved in social reform in an effort to lessen the gap between the rich and the poor. This involvement in social issues created conflicts between the bishops and government officials.

Although approximately 95 percent of Ecuadorians are said to be Roman Catholic, most Ecuadorians practice their religion only in the form of traditional holidays and festivities. In the Andes Highlands, particularly, the indigenous people have combined their native beliefs with many of the Catholic feasts, creating their own unique style of religious celebrations.

Below: **Catholic priests have worked to convert the native Ecuadorian population to Christianity since the mid-1500s.**

The Feast of San Juan

One celebration that combines Catholic and Indian themes is the Feast of San Juan, or St. John the Baptist. This holiday is an important celebration to the indigenous people of Ecuador. On June 24, people dress in beautiful, intricately designed costumes and dance in the streets. This particular festival began during the years of Incan rule as a celebration of the June solstice, which marks the longest day of the year.

Minority Religions

Minority religions in Ecuador, particularly Evangelical Christian groups, have increased in recent years. A multidenominational group known as the Gospel Missionary Union has been present in Ecuador since the beginning of the twentieth century. This group's missionaries go to remote areas of Ecuador to learn the Indian languages and the Indian lifestyle, and they have been successful in converting the native population in many rural areas, including Otavalo and several towns in Chimborazo.

Above: Catholic pilgrims pay their respects to the image of the Virgin at a church in Baños. The Virgin is said to perform miracles for pilgrims who seek her blessing.

Language and Literature

Referred to as *castellano* (kahs-teh-lee-AH-noh) by South Americans, Spanish is the official language of Ecuador. Castellano, the dialect spoken by the people of Castile in Spain, was brought to South America by the Spanish conquistadors in the 1500s. Almost all Ecuadorians speak this language. A smaller percentage of native Indians speak Quechua, the language of the Incas.

The Spanish alphabet is the same as the English alphabet, with the exception of three additional letters: *ch*, *ll*, and *ñ*.

In Ecuador, the way people speak Spanish changes from one region to another. The *costeños* (kohs-TEH-nee-ohs), or people living on the coast, speak very fast, whereas the *serranos* (seh-RAH-nohs), or people from the highlands, tend to speak slowly.

Below: **Magazines that published articles on social or political issues were banned in Ecuador by dictators in the past. Today, Ecuadorians enjoy freedom of the press.**

Left: **A bust of Juan Montalvo, a famous Ecuadorian writer of the nineteenth century, adorns the garden in front of Quito's House of Ecuadorian Culture.**

Literature

One of the most important Latin American writers of the nineteenth century, Juan Montalvo (1832–1889) wrote many essays criticizing the political situation in Ecuador. Although Montalvo served in his country's foreign service, he wrote many of his books while in exile because his criticism of the Ecuadorian government forced him to leave the country. Montalvo's most famous works are *The Seven Treatises* (1882) and *The Chapters that Cervantes Forgot* (1895).

Other important authors are Jorge Icaza (1906–1978) and Alicia Yáñez Cossio (1929–). Icaza initiated the "indigenous literature" movement in Ecuador with the publication of the novel *Huasipungo* in 1934. Yáñez Cossio is known for her lyrical narrative style. Her book *Bruna and Her Sisters in the Sleeping City* (1973) has received international acclaim.

COSTA VERSUS SIERRA

Although located side by side, the Coastal Lowland and the Andes Highlands of Ecuador are remarkably different from each other. The coast has warm weather and easygoing people. In contrast, the highlands have mostly cold weather and reserved people.

(A Closer Look, page 46)

Above: **The gold work on the entrance walls to Sagrario Church in Quito is an example of the artistry of colonial architecture.**

Arts

Spanish Legacy

During the colonial period, Spanish settlers built magnificent churches and government buildings throughout Quito and Cuenca. Many artists and sculptors embellished these churches with beautiful works of art. Seventeenth-century artist Miguel de Santiago and eighteenth-century sculptor Manuel Chili are known for their contributions to Ecuadorian colonial art. Both artists were trained in the style of the School of Quito. La Compañía de Jesús, a church in Quito, is an example of the architectural style of the 1600s.

Museums

Many museums throughout Quito showcase the works of famous Ecuadorian artists. The Guayasamín Museum houses a collection of pieces by Oswaldo Guayasamín (1919–1999), a world-famous

Ecuadorian painter. This museum is also home to many precolonial and colonial sculptures. Another museum, La Casa de la Cultura, is a pioneer in the development of the arts in Ecuador. Since its establishment in the 1940s, La Casa de la Cultura has sponsored artistic research, publications, and events through its many branches in cities around the country.

Indigenous Arts and Crafts

The native population of Ecuador created the country's earliest form of pottery. Archaeologists have found many ancient pieces dating as far back as 3500 B.C. Traditional crafts play a significant role in the lifestyle and economy of many Ecuadorians. Modern-day Ecuadorian craftspeople recreate some of these pieces of ancient pottery to sell as souvenirs to tourists. Each region sells unique crafts. The Indians of Otavalo create handmade wool products, including sweaters, jackets, and tapestries. Other areas that boast unique crafts are Ibarra, which is famous for its wood carvings, and Cotacachi, known for its leatherwork.

Below: The Indians of Otavalo make lovely handicrafts out of wool, such as these colorful dolls that are on sale at an open-air market in Otavalo.

Music

Each culture or ethnic group in Ecuador retains its own musical flavor. Ecuadorians express their feelings and emotions through music and lyrics. The older generation of Ecuadorians likes to sing and listen to songs that contain passionate expressions of love, life, and family. On the other hand, Ecuadorian youths take pleasure in listening to American music on the radio.

Andean Rhythms

The indigenous groups of Ecuador are known for their musical talent. These groups play upbeat tunes with only a few instruments. The main instruments used in traditional Andean folk tunes are the bamboo flute; the pan pipe; *charangos* (chah-RAHN-gohs), or small guitars; and drums. "Rosa María" and "El Cóndor Pasa" are two popular Andean folksongs. Andean people also enjoy dancing to the melancholic dance tunes of the *sanjuanitos* (sahn-who-ah-NEE-tohs).

Modern Ecuadorian music is influenced by the *cumbia* (KOOM-bee-ah) of Colombia, a dance rhythm that combines African and Caribbean tunes, and the salsa music of the Caribbean. Ecuadorian performers use rhythms inspired by these two styles to create their own tunes.

Above: **A group of street musicians plays Andean tunes with traditional instruments. In recent years, groups like this one have created a new musical style by mixing modern songs with Andean sounds.**

Marimba

Along the coast, in the city of Esmeraldas, Ecuadorians of African descent play a traditional instrument called the *marimba* (mah-REEM-bah). The marimba probably originated in South Africa. The top of the marimba resembles a keyboard, and pipes stem from the bottom. Ecuadorians of African descent like to gather at a "marimba house," where they celebrate a *currulao* (koo-roo-LAH-oh), or dance party, by singing and dancing to African rhythms on the marimba.

Amazon Rhythms

Amazon Jungle dwellers perform a warrior dance called the "Spirit of the Anaconda." The musicians play instruments made of materials found in the rain forest, such as turtle shells and bamboo rattles. Both men and women dancers wear traditional grass skirts and, through song and dance, tell the story of the anaconda, a very large and powerful snake native to the Amazon Jungle.

Below: Ecuadorian Indians celebrate the feast of Corpus Christi by dressing up in colorful costumes and dancing in the streets.

Leisure and Festivals

Ecuadorians enjoy spending their leisure time in parks, playing sports, or having picnics. At home, Ecuadorians of all ages like to watch *telenovelas* (teh-leh-noh-VEH-lahs), or soap operas. Similar to the North American soap opera, telenovelas are a dramatic version of life in Latin America. Many Ecuadorians adjust their schedules in order to set aside time to watch their favorite telenovela. Ecuadorians who live near the coast spend much of their free time at the beach.

Ecuadorians in larger cities, such as Quito and Guayaquil, enjoy the same kinds of entertainment as North Americans. Restaurants and clubs are available for fine dining and entertaining. Movie theaters show the latest releases from Hollywood. Internet usage is also common among Ecuadorians. On weekends, many youths spend their time at discos, dancing to North American and salsa music. Most of these activities are enjoyed mainly by the upper classes, however.

SEMANA SANTA

Ecuadorians celebrate *Semana Santa* (seh-MAH-nah SAHN-tah), or Easter, in a variety of ways. Many of the Catholic religious traditions brought by the Spaniards have been mixed with native Indian beliefs, creating unique forms of celebration.
(A Closer Look, page 72)

Left: An Ecuadorian family, including their native Indian housekeeper and her children, enjoys a picnic at one of the many parks in Quito.

OTAVALO

Surrounded by the Andes Mountains and beautiful lakes, the city of Otavalo is famous for its unique handicrafts. The lovely wool garments, colorful textiles, and wood carvings of the Otavalo Indians are highly regarded in Ecuador and abroad.

(A Closer Look, page 64)

Left: The beauty queen of the Flower and Fruit Festival waves at the crowd during the festival's main parade.

Children's Games

Most Ecuadorian children enjoy simple games such as marbles, jump rope, and hopscotch. They often play games that do not require any special equipment. Ecuadorian children also like to use their imagination to create guessing games and rhymes. One such game involves making up and singing new, original lyrics for popular songs.

Beauty Pageants

Beauty pageants are popular throughout Latin America, including Ecuador. Unlike the traditional pageants in North America, pageants in Ecuador are much less formal in manner. All levels of society enjoy these contests, which are usually held during special holidays and celebrations.

Sports

Soccer is the most popular sport in Ecuador. Called *fútbol* (FOOT-bohl) in Ecuador, it is also the national sport. Men and boys organize teams and spend much of their free time on the soccer field. Almost every town in Ecuador has a soccer team. Ecuadorian women enjoy tennis, basketball, volleyball, and track and field. For people who enjoy water sports, many resorts along the coast offer surfing, scuba diving, and windsurfing instruction. Since practicing water sports is expensive, these resorts are limited, for the most part, to wealthy Ecuadorians and tourists.

Below: **A group of young Ecuadorians plays a game of ecua-volley at El Ejido Park in Quito.**

Ecua-volley

Another favorite sport is *ecua-volley* (EH-koo-ah-BOH-lay), the Ecuadorian form of volleyball. This sport is especially popular in the Andes Highlands. Unlike traditional volleyball, ecua-volley has only three players on each team.

Pelota Nacional

An interesting game called *pelota nacional* (peh-LOH-tah nah-see-oh-NAHL) is enjoyed by Ecuadorians of all ages. Pelota requires three teams, a team on each end of the playing field and one team in the middle. The team in the middle tries to keep the other two teams from hitting the ball back and forth. People playing this game are common sights in parks around Quito.

Sports Stars

Ecuador is the proud home of several talented athletes who have made their mark in international competitions. Over the years, soccer idol Alex Aguinaga has increased Ecuadorians' love for the sport with his talent and prowess. Born in Ibarra, Aguinaga has played professional soccer since he was sixteen years old. Aguinaga is considered to be the key player in ensuring a place

Below: Ecuadorian boys play the nation's favorite sport at a soccer field located 10,000 feet (3,048 m) above sea level.

for Ecuador in the 2002 World Cup championship to be held in Japan and South Korea. If the Ecuadorian national team qualifies, Ecuador will be competing for the first time in the World Cup.

Jefferson Pérez, a native of Cuenca, is the first Ecuadorian to win a gold medal at the Olympic Games. Pérez won the gold medal for race walking at the 1996 Olympic Games in Atlanta. Pérez has also won first place in other international events, such as the Pan-American Games and the World Cup of race walking.

Tennis pro Nicolás Lapentti, another Ecuadorian sports legend, was ranked by Wimbledon 2000 as number ten out of the twenty best players at Wimbledon.

NICOLÁS LAPENTTI

Ecuador's biggest tennis star, Nicolás Lapentti started playing tennis at the age of seven. Today, "Nico" is among the top twenty best tennis players in the world.
(A Closer Look, page 62)

Festivals

The Ecuadorian calendar overflows with religious, government, and local holidays. Ecuadorian festivals are related to Catholic celebrations, although many of these festivals have their origins in Indian traditions. Catholic and native traditions have merged to create uniquely Ecuadorian celebrations.

New Year's Day

Ecuadorians welcome the new year and leave the old year behind with a traditional ritual. For this event, Ecuadorians make a mannequin that represents the events of the past year. At midnight, the mannequin is burned to the ground to symbolize a fresh start.

National Day

Ecuadorians celebrate National Day on August 10, with parades, food, music, and dance. Guayaquil holds a celebration for its own independence day as well, on October 9.

Left: Ecuadorian Indians take part in a parade to celebrate the Catholic feast of Corpus Christi.

Carnaval

Carnival, or *Carnaval* (kahr-nah-VAHL), in Ecuador traditionally begins three days before Ash Wednesday, which usually falls in February, but celebrations may start before that. Ecuadorians celebrate Carnaval by dressing in colorful costumes and taking part in parades and masked parties. Ecuadorians also celebrate by throwing water balloons at one another. During these festivities, people on the street must be on the alert to avoid getting soaked by youngsters hiding behind doors, waiting for their next "water target" to walk by.

Above: **People from Otavalo carry the statue of St. John during the Feast of San Juan, or St. John the Baptist.**

Día de los Muertos

The Ecuadorian version of All Saints Day, *Día de los Muertos* (DEE-ah deh lohs moo-EHR-tohs), on November 2, is a day when Ecuadorians visit the graves of their loved ones. On this "day of the dead," Ecuadorians prepare a drink made from blue corn and berries. The drink, called *colada morada* (koh-LAH-dah moh-RAH-dah), is enjoyed with bread rolls. In the Sierra, people take food to the cemetery and eat near the graves of their loved ones.

Food

Exotic fruits, abundant vegetables, and a large variety of seafood — all are readily available for locals and visitors in Ecuador. Most towns in the country even have their own traditional dishes.

Ecuadorian Meals

Most Ecuadorians eat three meals a day. Breakfast is small, perhaps a bread or sweet roll and a hot drink, such as tea or coffee. Lunch, the biggest meal of the day, includes at least two courses. Ecuadorians always begin lunch with a bowl of soup, which is followed by the main dish of meat, rice or potatoes, and a salad. Dessert is a type of flan, which is similar to pudding. The evening meal is usually similar to lunch but in smaller portions. In between lunch and dinner, Ecuadorians sometimes enjoy tasty snacks, such as *empanadas* (ehm-pah-NAH-dahs), hot, crispy pastries with meat or cheese fillings.

Below: Ceviche (seh-VEE-cheh), **a tangy, delicious dish made of raw fish marinated in a lemon sauce, is one of Ecuador's most popular coastal dishes.**

Typical Ecuadorian Cuisine

Along the coast, seafood dishes are popular. Ceviche, raw fish or seafood marinated in citrus juice and seasoned with onion, is a special favorite. In the Andes Highlands, people prepare *cuy* (KOO-ee), or baked guinea pig. Staple foods in Ecuador include rice; *yuca* (YOO-kah), a vegetable similar to the potato; plantains; and potatoes. Some combination of these staples is served at nearly every meal. Plantains can be fried, boiled, or baked to make anything from chips to dessert. These particular foods are significant to the Ecuadorian diet because they are nutritious and economical.

Chili Sauce

An Ecuadorian meal would not be complete without a dab of *ají* (ah-HEE) to spice up the meal. Ají, or chili, grows in many different varieties in Ecuador. Ecuadorians pound the chilis and add a bit of water and seasonings to the mixture to make a sauce. Most homes and restaurants in Ecuador make their own ají sauces.

Above: Savory snacks, such as plantain chips, are available at street stalls in most major cities in Ecuador.

STREET SNACKS

Food vendors are common sights in towns and cities throughout Ecuador. These vendors prepare and sell a popular snack called *salchi-papas* (SAHL-chee-PAH-pahs), a small dish of french fries and pieces of sausage. Other snacks sold by street vendors are barbecued corn and pork.

A CLOSER LOOK AT ECUADOR

Ecuador is home to distinct and separate cultures whose traditions and lifestyles are not found anywhere else in the world. These groups of people live in both the small and large cities that dot Ecuador.

Quito stands tall in the highlands as an ancient Incan city and as the colonial capital. The native peoples of Otavalo and Cuenca in the Andes are two indigenous cultures that have kept their values and traditions while adapting to the changing environment of modern Ecuador. Along the coast, small groups of native Indians perform daily chores in the same manner their ancestors did hundreds of years ago. Beyond the coast, the Galápagos Islands are an awesome example of unspoiled nature and home to the largest tortoise species in the world. Ecuador is working hard to preserve the natural environment of these islands and other endangered areas through nature conservation efforts. Although small in land area, Ecuador is a country of diverse peoples and cultures, as well as breathtaking and unique landscapes.

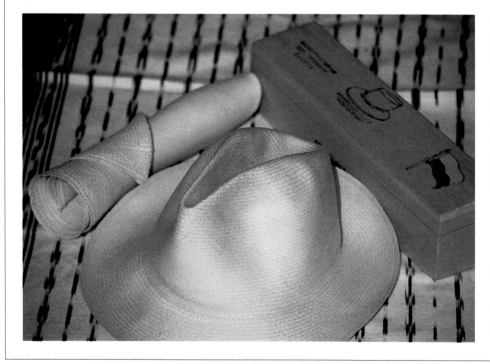

Opposite: **The government palace in Quito, known as the Carondelet Palace, was originally built to house the Spanish colonial government. The palace has been used as Ecuador's official seat of government since the country's independence from Spain in the 1820s.**

Left: **The Panama hat is one of Ecuador's most famous handicrafts and the main source of revenue for many Ecuadorian artisans.**

The Amazon Jungle

The Amazon Jungle of Ecuador boasts more biodiversity than any other place on Earth. The Ecuadorian Amazon is home to 10 percent of all the tree species found in the world and nearly 18 percent of all known bird species. The Amazon rain forest is also inhabited by small groups of native peoples.

Yasuni National Park

The Yasuni National Park, located in the province of Orellana, exhibits an impressive variety of wildlife, including anacondas, king buzzards, macaws and numerous other colorful birds, dolphins, boars, and monkeys. The plant life is equally impressive, with peanut, cinnamon, and balsa trees. Tourist trails run through thick, green forests with trees towering to 150 feet (46 m). Two groups of Huaorani Indians live within the boundaries of the park. The Huaorani keep mostly to themselves and avoid contact with people outside their community.

Below: **The water from the San Rafael Falls, located in the eastern chain of the Andes Mountains, flows into the Coca River.**

Left: **A Huaorani woman weaves strings of cotton to make a hammock.**

A Delicate Ecosystem

In recent years, many oil and lumber companies have tried to take advantage of the enormous natural resources the rain forest has to offer. These companies have built roads and cut down many trees, causing great damage to the environment. The rain forest is a delicate ecosystem of plants and animals that depend on each other to survive. Cutting down even one tree may deprive hundreds of animals and insects of a home or food. In an effort to protect the Ecuadorian Amazon Jungle, the president of Ecuador blocked oil exploration and mining of certain areas around Cuyabeno and the Yasuni National Park in 1999.

Amazon Indians

Conflict between the Amazon Indians and the Ecuadorian government over land use has existed for many years. To find a solution to this conflict, Ecuadorian president Rodrigo Borja Cevallos granted land titles to over 3 million acres (1,214,100 hectares), mostly in the province of Pastaza, to the Amazon Indians in 1992. Amazon Indian leaders, dressed in traditional attire, attended a special ceremony at the presidential palace to receive the land titles, which prohibit development of the areas without the consent of the community. This land grant is one of the largest concessions made to the Amazon Indians by any South American government.

Costa versus Sierra

Ecuadorian people often comment on the differences between the Costa and the Sierra. The character and lifestyles of the people from the coast and the people of the Andes are strongly influenced by the climate and land features of the two regions.

The Costa

The coast of Ecuador is a wide, flat plain that consists of miles (km) of beaches from Esmeraldas to Salinas and beyond. The weather on the coast is hot and humid. The people who live on the coast, known as costeños, work mostly on farms or plantations. Because of the heat, costeños wear very light clothing most of the time. Children spend much of their time barefoot, wearing only shorts and T-shirts. Most costeños lead an easygoing lifestyle. Dance parties are common along the coast. Costeños eat food typical to the coast, mostly fish and fruit. They also eat fried plantains and rice flavored with onions or tomatoes.

Below: **A group of costeños enjoys a day at Salinas beach.**

The Sierra

The majority of the Ecuadorian population lives in the Sierra. Serranos, or people from the Andes Highlands, lead a completely different lifestyle from the costeños. Most serranos who live in large cities, such as Quito, have a more fast-paced lifestyle. Generally speaking, the serranos tend to be private people and are not as outgoing or outspoken as the costeños. The conservative nature of the serranos is partly a result of the climate. Nights are usually very cold in the Sierra, making it difficult to hold large fiestas outdoors. Major cities in the Sierra include Quito, Otavalo, Ibarra, Cayambe, Ambato, and Cuenca.

The Sierra is also more technologically advanced than the Costa. *Quiteños* (kee-TEH-nee-ohs), or people from Quito, have more access to modern technology, including the Internet, than people on the coast. The more prestigious schools and universities are also located in the Sierra.

People in the Sierra enjoy eating typical Andean produce. Potatoes, corn, and yuca are the main staples. They also eat baked guinea pig, or cuy, on special occasions and celebrations.

Despite their differences, Ecuadorians have one voice when it comes to their land and their customs. Ecuadorians from every region take pride in their history and traditions.

Above: **Native Indians quietly and diligently plow the land near the slopes of Chimborazo Volcano northwest of Riobamba.**

Cuenca

Located in southern central Ecuador, Cuenca, the capital of Azuay Province, is Ecuador's third largest city. The city is a commercial center, and its open-air markets are well known throughout Ecuador. The Spaniards founded Cuenca in 1557 on the ruins of a former Incan city. Since then, Cuenca has been a commercial city and the birthplace of many artists and craftspeople.

The city of Cuenca resembles a park, with many green areas, rivers, and brooks running through the city. The cobblestone streets are a reminder of the Spanish colonial era, yet the people here lead a distinctive and conservative Andean lifestyle.

Cuenca enjoys temperate, springlike weather all year round. The temperature ranges from 40° to 50° F (4° to 10° C) at night to 60° to 70° F (15° to 21° C) during the day. This ideal weather contributes to the growing flower cultivation business aimed at the export market.

Below: **The Cathedral of the Virgin of the Immaculate Conception in Cuenca stands amid the city's government buildings.**

Open-Air Markets

Open-air markets in Cuenca boast a colorful array of exotic fruits and vegetables. Fresh meats, fish, and homemade breads are also sold at these markets. World-famous Panama hats, textiles and lace, leather goods, and jewelry attract locals and tourists to the markets every week. Merchants sell unique herbal teas, native grains, and numerous medicinal foods. Some of these herbal teas serve as a cure for *soroche* (soh-ROH-chay), or altitude sickness. The cinchona tree, which produces quinine, grows in great numbers in Cuenca.

Important Buildings

The ancient Indian ruins of Inga Pirca are located near Cuenca. Many colonial structures built under Spanish rule still stand in the city. Although the large plantations were divided and sold in pieces, some of the old, beautiful homes owned by wealthy landowners still remain, and many of them have been turned into museums. Cuenca is home to two beautiful cathedrals, a government palace, and two universities.

Above: **Native Indians from Cuenca show off their crafts at one of the city's markets.**

PANAMA HATS

Cuenca is a major producer of Panama hats, or *jipijapa* (hee-pee-HAH-pah), which were first produced in the town of Jipijapa in Manabi Province. Although Ecuador has produced Panama hats for centuries, the hat took its name from the port city that once shipped the hats to every corner of the world. U.S. president Teddy Roosevelt and England's King Edward VII made the Ecuadorian hat part of their attire.

Dollarization

In the late 1990s, Ecuador's declining economy and unstable governments forced Ecuadorian officials to take drastic measures for economic recovery. On January 9, 2000, the government of Ecuador declared the U.S. dollar the legal tender, a process called "dollarization." This move was made in an effort to stop inflation and stabilize the exchange rate. The U.S. dollar replaced the sucre, the former currency of Ecuador, as Ecuador's official currency.

Historical Factors

Several external factors contributed to the major economic crisis Ecuador faced in 1999. The drop in oil prices; the effects of the El Niño phenomenon on the weather, which devastated crops; and the Asian and Brazilian economic crises, as well as Ecuador's political instability plunged the country into a crisis.

On March 2, 1999, the Ecuadorian government forced the banks to close and froze all accounts. Throughout the rest of the year, Ecuador experienced a deep recession. Ecuador was not able to pay the money it owed to other countries, and the government could not reach an agreement with the international financial institutions to renegotiate the debts.

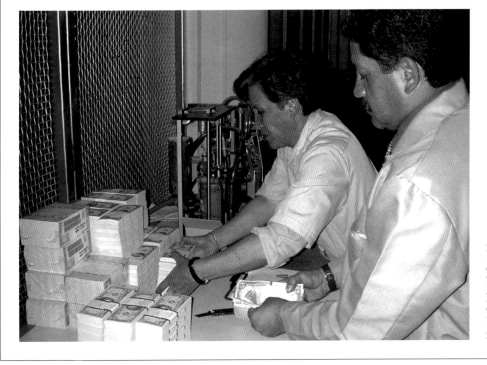

Left: Workers at Ecuador's Central Bank classify U.S. dollar bills as part of the preparation for the dollarization of the Ecuadorian currency in April 2000.

Dollarization of the Sucre

When President Jamil Mahuad proposed dollarization on January 9, 2000, most Ecuadorians accepted the idea. However, when the government informed Ecuadorians of the exchange rate of 25,000 sucres for U.S. $1, Ecuadorians were infuriated. Some people had deposited money in the bank when the exchange rate was 6,000 sucres to $1, so their deposits had depreciated by 400 percent. Protests and riots followed, and within days, Mahuad was forced to flee the presidential palace. Gustavo Noboa, Mahuad's vice president, replaced Mahuad. Noboa, a supporter of dollarization, continued with the proposal.

Effects of Dollarization

Although initial reactions toward dollarization were mixed, the change has so far been beneficial to the Ecuadorian economy. In April 2000, Ecuador reached an agreement with the International Monetary Fund (IMF) to negotiate new loans. Inflation has decreased significantly, and foreign investment has increased. As of March 2001, 98 percent of the sucres in Ecuador have been replaced by the U.S. dollar. The government has begun to pay wages and collect taxes in U.S. dollars.

Above: **Many Ecuadorians bought U.S. dollars from street traders when dollarization took effect because the traders offered a better exchange rate than the banks.**

Ecuador–Peru Border Conflict

A long-standing border conflict between Ecuador and Peru escalated on January 26, 1995, when an Ecuadorian helicopter bombed a Peruvian army post in the disputed area on Ecuador's southern border. Ecuador's position was that the Rio Protocol of 1942, which had conceded the disputed area to Peru, had drawn the border based on inaccurate topographical information, making the border specifications invalid. The disputed area is located mainly in the province of Zamora-Chinchipe.

Historical Background

Tension between Ecuador and Peru over Ecuador's southern provinces had existed since Ecuador's independence from Spain in 1822. Ecuador's initial weakness as a young republic ruled by unstable governments made Ecuador's borders vulnerable to invasions by Colombia and Peru.

Below: Ecuadorian troops in tanks patrol the streets of a town near the disputed area between Ecuador and Peru in the province of Zamora-Chinchipe.

The Rio Protocol

In 1942, the Protocol of Peace, Friendship, and Boundaries was signed in Rio de Janeiro by Ecuador, Peru, Argentina, Brazil, Chile, and the United States to put an end to the war that had broken out between Ecuador and Peru in 1941. This treaty granted the disputed area to Peru, forcing Ecuador to give up about 77,000 square miles (199,430 square km) of land. The Rio Protocol, however, did not clearly demarcate an area along approximately 48 miles (77 km) of the eastern slopes of the Condor mountain range. Many Ecuadorians felt that the treaty was invalid because it had demarcated the border between Ecuador and Peru based on inaccurate geographical data.

Above: **Ecuadorian president Jamil Mahuad (*left*) and Peruvian president Alberto Fujimori (*right*) smile at a press conference held after signing the Acta de Brasilia treaty, named after the city where the treaty was signed.**

Peace Agreement

In February 1995, Ecuadorian and Peruvian forces agreed to stop the fighting. The four countries that had signed the Rio Protocol established the Military Observers Mission to Ecuador–Peru (MOMEP) to monitor the area. In 1996, representatives from Ecuador and Peru began a series of meetings to resolve the dispute. On October 26, 1998, Ecuadorian president Jamil Mahuad and Peruvian president Alberto Fujimori signed an historic peace agreement in Brasilia, Brazil.

Famous Sites

Ecuador is home to many world-famous sites that date from the time of the Incan civilization and the Spanish colonial period. Ecuador also boasts breathtaking natural land formations that tourists come to view.

El Panecillo

A beautiful statue of the Virgin of Quito stands high upon *El Panecillo* (ehl pah-neh-SEEL-loh), or "little bread loaf," Hill. Museums, churches, town squares, and an Indian market are found in the Old City district of Quito at the base of El Panecillo.

La Mitad del Mundo

The monument La Mitad del Mundo, which means "Half of the World," is located at the equator, exactly 0 degrees latitude, 14 miles (22.5 km) north of Quito. In 1736, an expedition led by French explorer Charles-Marie de la Condamine (1701–1774) determined the exact location.

Below: **A charming old street lined with colonial buildings winds its way to El Panecillo Hill in Quito.**

Avenue of Volcanoes

The Avenue of Volcanoes is a beautiful valley extending from southern Quito to Cuenca. The two parallel mountain ranges that flank the valley include nine of the highest mountain peaks in Ecuador. The Pan-American Highway makes travel along the valley accessible and enjoyable and provides incredible views of volcanoes, as well as a look at small Indian villages along the way. Along this route, Ambato, the city of flowers, and the towering Tungurahua Volcano are popular tourist stops.

Above: **Cotopaxi, the world's highest active volcano, is one of the most impressive sights along the Avenue of Volcanoes.**

Monastery of San Francisco

The Monastery of San Francisco in Quito, a church built in the sixteenth century, is the largest colonial structure in Ecuador, as well as the oldest church in the country. Franciscan missionary Jodoco Ricke began the construction of the monastery shortly after Rumiñahui burned the city to the ground. The Monastery of San Francisco took many years to complete, and the final touches were made around the turn of the seventeenth century. Experts have repaired the monastery on several occasions because of damage caused by earthquakes.

Galápagos Islands

The Galápagos Islands are a group of thirteen main islands and many small islets located 620 miles (1,000 km) off the Ecuadorian coast. In 1832, the islands were annexed by Ecuador and are officially known in Spanish as the Archipiélago de Colón. The name *galápagos* (gah-LAH-pah-gohs) comes from the old Spanish name for the giant tortoises that live on the islands. The Galápagos Islands have a land area of 3,093 square miles (8,010 square km). The largest island, Isabela, covers most of that area.

Left: The striking contrast between the volcanic, ash-colored terrain of Santiago, on the island of San Salvador, and the sparkling blue waters around the island is a sight unique to the Galápagos Islands.

CHARLES DARWIN

Charles Darwin, an English naturalist, visited the Galápagos Islands in 1835. Darwin observed that many of the birds on the islands differed only in beak shape and size. Darwin concluded that the birds shared one common ancestor, but that, in order to survive, these birds had been forced to adapt to their particular environments over thousands of years. Darwin presented these ideas on natural selection in his book *On the Origin of Species* (1859).

Amazing Plant and Animal Life

The Galápagos Islands support about 700 species of plants, of which 40 percent are unique to the islands. The tall variety of the prickly pear cactus grows on the arid lowlands. Many of the plants on the Galápagos Islands are closely related to plants in Central and South America.

The animal life on the Galápagos is extraordinary. Most of the animals are endemic, or found only in the Galápagos. These animals include blue-footed boobies, sea lions, finches, giant tortoises, iguanas, and penguins. Tropical animals, such as iguanas, and Antarctic animals, such as penguins, live side by side on the islands.

Danger in the Galápagos

Uncontrolled tourism, the introduction of nonnative animal and plant species to the islands, and an increase in the human population are threatening the survival of the environment on the Galápagos Islands. The Ecuadorian government and numerous international organizations have set up environmental restrictions to protect the endemic species of these islands.

Above: Male land iguanas on the Galápagos live near the seashore.

Below: The lightfoot crab is endemic to the Galápagos Islands.

The Giant Tortoise

The giant tortoise of the Galápagos Islands is the largest living tortoise in the world, weighing more than 500 pounds (227 kilograms). The giant tortoise has the longest life span of any creature on Earth. Some of the tortoises found on the Galápagos Islands today are believed to have hatched at the time Charles Darwin visited the islands in the 1830s.

Tortoise Lifestyle

Native to the Galápagos Islands, the giant tortoise enjoys a volcanic island habitat. The tortoise likes to spend the cooler part of the day in the dry lowlands and the warmer part of the day in the highlands, feeding on fresh plant life. The life span of a tortoise can be anywhere between 100 and 200 years. The female giant tortoise lays two to sixteen eggs at a time and digs a large hole in which to bury them. The incubation period can last from three to eight months depending on the weather. In warm weather, the incubation takes less time than in cool weather. The mother tortoise does not raise the babies; the babies must fend for themselves from the time they hatch. Giant tortoises have very regular habits. They choose a particular spot to sleep and eat, and females nest in the same place year after year.

Left: **A giant tortoise in the Galápagos treads its way across the island of Santa Cruz.**

Through the Charles Darwin Foundation, a research and rescue station has been set up on the island of Santa Cruz in the Galápagos to increase the survival rate of the giant tortoise. Eggs from giant tortoises are incubated at the research station, and the baby tortoises are raised until they are four or five years old. Ecuador has passed laws protecting the giant tortoise from being captured or exported.

Left: The famous English naturalist Charles Darwin first visited the Galápagos Islands during a trip made aboard the ship *The Beagle* in 1835 at the age of twenty-four.

In Danger of Extinction

The giant tortoise is in danger of becoming extinct. When Darwin visited the Galápagos Islands, the number of giant tortoises was nearly 250,000; today, only about 15,000 giant tortoises live on the islands. Over the years, the giant tortoise population has decreased sharply due to a number of factors. The tortoise was a major source of food for sailors, who took the creatures on board because of the tortoises' ability to live for a long period of time without food or water. Sailors would stack the tortoises in the cargo area and keep the animals as a source of fresh meat. Also, animals that have been introduced to the islands, such as rats and cats, have eaten many of the tortoises' eggs over the years.

Guayaquil

Guayaquil is Ecuador's largest city and main seaport. Located along the southern coast of Ecuador, Guayaquil is an expanding metropolis and the country's import and export hub. The Guayas River runs through Guayaquil. The city is located on the river's western bank. *Guayaquileños* (goo-ah-yah-kee-LAY-nee-ohs), or people from Guayaquil, are proud of their city's heritage. People from other parts of Ecuador flock to Guayaquil to attend the city's several prestigious universities and polytechnics and also to find jobs, since Guayaquil offers more job opportunities than any other city in Ecuador. Guayaquil has a population of over 2 million people.

Historical Background

Guayaquil was founded in 1535 by Spaniard conquistador Sebastián de Benalcázar. The city takes its name from an Indian chief, Guaya, who ruled Guayaquil before the arrival of the

Below: **The street Malecón Simón Bolívar in Guayaquil is named after one of the country's liberators.**

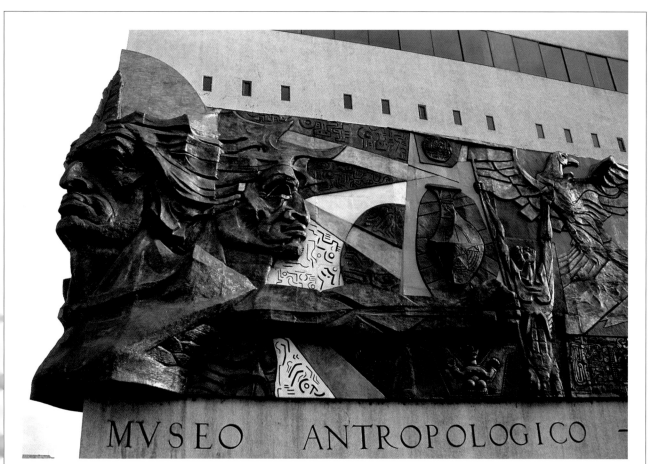

MVSEO ANTROPOLOGICO

Spaniards, and the chief's wife, Quila. Guayaquil was burned down twice by the native Indians and rebuilt by the Spaniards. In 1820, an army of Guayaquileños claimed independence from Spain even before Simón Bolívar annexed Ecuador to the confederation of La Gran Colombia. Every year, the city celebrates its own independence day on October 9.

Above: **A modern mural adorns the building of the Central Bank in Guayaquil, which also houses the city's Anthropological Museum.**

Popular Spots

Guayaquileños are known for their entrepreneurial spirit. One recent project designed to boost Ecuador's economy is "El Malecón 2000." El Malecón Avenue, a street that runs parallel to the Guayas River, is now lined with restaurants, theaters, and parks that aim to attract shoppers and tourists to Guayaquil.

A favorite weekend retreat for Guayaquileños is Playas, a beach lined with seafood restaurants and ceviche stands. Other beaches along the Santa Elena Peninsula, such as Salinas beach, cater to tourists and the Ecuadorian upper classes by offering activities such as yachting and deep-sea fishing.

Nicolás Lapentti

Nicolás Lapentti, known to his fans as "Nico," is currently a top-class tennis player and the pride of Guayaquil, as well as Ecuador as a whole. Lapentti began playing tennis at the age of seven and played in the junior categories at the French Open and the U.S. Open Juniors. Lapentti won the Orange Bowl in 1994 in his first year as a professional player.

Lapentti's Early Years

Nicolás Lapentti was born on August 13, 1976, in Guayaquil and became a professional tennis player at the age of nineteen. Although Lapentti travels extensively to participate in tennis matches, his permanent residence remains in Guayaquil. A typical Guayaquileño, Lapentti enjoys soccer and reads Robert Ludlum books in his spare time. Patricio Rodriguez, a former professional tennis player, is Lapentti's coach. Lapentti's younger brother, Giovanni, is also a professional tennis player.

Left: **Ecuador's tennis star "Nico" Lapentti plays against American Pete Sampras at the Ericsson Open held in Australia in March 2000. Sampras eventually won the match in a tie breaker.**

Lapentti's Professional Record

Lapentti holds three singles titles and three doubles titles and has a record of 169 wins to 137 losses in his professional career. Lapentti represented his country at the 1996 Olympic Games in Atlanta. In January 2001, Lapentti competed in the Australian Open, winning three doubles events and one singles event. Lapentti has played against such international tennis stars as Pete Sampras and Andre Agassi.

Father and Son

Lapentti's achievements are a result of sacrifice and self-discipline. The tennis player's work ethic and athletic prowess were significantly influenced by Lapentti's father, who was a great basketball player. His father loved sports and passed his passion for athletics on to his son. During Lapentti's early years as a tennis player, his father worked hard to get sponsors to support his son's matches abroad. Never forgetting his own beginnings, in January 2001, Lapentti established a sports foundation for the youth of Ecuador.

Above: **Nicolás Lapentti** *(right)* **and his brother Giovanni** *(left)* **compete as a doubles team against Arvind Parmar and Tim Henman at the 2000 Davis Cup.**

Otavalo

The traditions and lifestyles of the Otavalan people are a source of pride in Ecuador. The people of Otavalo are indigenous to Ecuador and refer to themselves as "pure" native Indians. Otavalo is located about 68 miles (110 km) north of Quito in a valley surrounded by the Andes Mountains and San Pablo, Mojanda, and Yahuarcocha lakes.

The Otavalan People

Otavalans are different from any other group of people in Ecuador. The Otavalans can be distinguished by their traditional dress, which consists of a white shirt, pants, and a type of slipper for the men and a beautifully embroidered blouse and a long, dark, straight skirt for the women. The women also wear golden beads around their neck. Most Otavalan women and men wear their hair long and tied in a braid.

THE OTAVALAN MARKETPLACE

The marketplace in Otavalo is a wonderful showcase for the talents and handicrafts of the Otavalans. Otavalans gather here from every part of the city to sell their crafts. The busiest days at the market are Saturdays and Sundays. The bustling daily market not only attracts Ecuadorians, but it is also a popular attraction for tourists.

Left: An elderly Otavalan woman is busy working at her colorful tapestry stall at the market.

Hardworking Otavalans

Otavalans are a hardworking and industrious people. They are also one of the few native peoples of Ecuador who have achieved economic success through the sale of their handicrafts in Ecuador and abroad. Much of the profit earned by the Otavalans in the marketplace comes from the selling of their products to European and North American tourists.

Above: **Beautiful Mojanda Lake is one of a number of scenic lakes and lagoons found near Otavalo.**

Folk Arts

The beautiful handicrafts produced by the Otavalan people include wool items, such as sweaters, jackets, hats, gloves, and socks; silver accessories, such as rings, necklaces, and earrings; a great variety of textiles; and wood carvings. A popular Otavalan carving is the figure of an elderly man who is either sitting on a bench or holding a cane. Otavalans are also famous for their distinct music. Otavalan musicians play mainly wooden flutes. Otavalan music groups have performed their unique melodies in many countries around the world.

Prehistory

Some of the oldest remains of ancient civilizations in the American continents have been found in Ecuador. Major archaeological sites are found in the provinces of Manabi and Esmeraldas along the coast; Carchi, Imbabura, Tungurahua, and Chimborazo in the Andes Highlands; and Cañar, Azuay, and Loja in the southern part of Ecuador.

Artifacts found at these sites date back to thousands of years before the Inca Empire conquered Ecuador in the 1400s. Although no actual structures from pre-Incan cultures remain standing, archaeologists have studied the artifacts, such as pottery and metal objects, found at the sites, and they have learned a great deal about the way the people of these ancient cultures lived. Most of the artifacts from these ancient Ecuadorian civilizations are on display at the Museos del Banco Central, or Ecuador's Central Bank Museums, located in Quito, Guayaquil, and Cuenca.

INGA PIRCA

Inga Pirca is the best-preserved Incan site in Ecuador. It is located about a day's trip from Cuenca in the province of Cañar. Inga Pirca was a religious site, and the site consists of a complex of courtyards, homes, terraces, and a sun temple. A museum on the site exhibits archaeological remains of the Inca Empire, such as ceramics, jewelry, and textiles.

Left: This sculpture from La Tolita culture was made between the years 500 B.C. and A.D. 500. The sculpture represents a male serpent.

Left: **La Tolita culture is famous for crafting beautiful objects out of metal, such as this gold sun mask.**

Valdivia Culture

The earliest indication of a settlement in Ecuador dates back to as early as 3500 B.C. The Valdivia culture, which flourished between 3500 and 1500 B.C. along the coast in the provinces of Guayas and Manabi, has left some examples of beautiful pottery and sculpture. The sculptures include female figurines crafted with great artistic talent and attention to detail. Some evidence suggests that the Valdivia culture also built ceremonial temples.

La Tolita and Manta Cultures

Other early civilizations were those of La Tolita and Manta. Flourishing around 300 B.C., La Tolita culture was a prosperous civilization along the Pacific coast in Esmeraldas Province. This culture is famous for intricate gold carvings, such as figurines and ornaments. The Manta culture, found in the province of Manabi, built large cities. Experts believe that the Manta culture had over 20,000 members at one time. This culture has left behind pottery, objects made of gold and silver, and some pieces made out of stone.

Quito

Nestled in the Andean Mountains nearly 10,000 feet (3,048 m) above sea level, Quito is the capital city of Ecuador. Snowcapped mountains nearby and a temperate climate make Quito an attractive and pleasant place to live. Quito is home to a diverse group of people. While the majority of the people are considered mestizos, or people with mixed Spanish and Indian ancestry, Europeans, North Americans, Asians, and indigenous people also reside side by side in Quito.

Below: **Plaza Indoamérica in Quito displays large statues of native Indian leaders, a reminder of the city's past.**

Quito's "Four Seasons"

Ecuador is endowed with rich and unique geographical features, and the city of Quito is one great example of this uniqueness. Quito is home to beautiful mountains and an active volcano. Due to the city's high elevation, yet central location on the equator, the temperature remains relatively constant the whole year round. On average, the days are sunny and warm, and the nights are cool. Quito's rainy season begins in November and usually lasts until March. Some say that in Quito you can count all four seasons in one day: spring in the morning, summer in the afternoon, fall in the late afternoon, and winter at night.

Quito's Early Days

Quito was once the cradle of numerous ancient Indian civilizations, and each one of these cultures has left its mark on the city's cultural heritage. Beginning in the twelfth century, Quito was the capital of the Cara civilization led by the Shyri dynasty. During the fifteenth century, Quito served as the capital of the Quitus culture. The Inca Empire took over Quito and annexed the city in the sixteenth century. During the last years of Incan rule, when the Spaniards arrived in Ecuador, Rumiñahui, an Incan general, burned and demolished Quito in an effort to prevent the invaders from taking over the city.

A Capital City

After the Spaniards conquered the Inca Empire, Quito was rebuilt by Spanish lieutenant Sebastián de Benalcázar, and the city became one of the seats of the Spanish colonial government in South America. Today, the city of Quito is divided into two sections. The Old City is remarkably well-preserved. Beautiful examples of Spanish colonial architecture line the streets. In fact, Quito is one of the best preserved Spanish colonial cities in South America. The New City, on the other hand, is a modern city in every sense, with towering office buildings, hotels, restaurants, and modern museums.

Above: **The Guapulo Cathedral in Quito, built between 1644 and 1693, sits at the edge of a ravine.**

Saving the Environment

In a country such as Ecuador, which has such an extensive variety of plant and animal life, programs to protect the ecosystem are extremely important. The government has set up comprehensive programs throughout Ecuador for plant and wildlife conservation. These programs provide environmental education for young people and adults.

Jatun Sacha

Jatun Sacha, a private, nonprofit Ecuadorian foundation, was established in 1989. The foundation employs volunteers to educate people about the environment and to work on

GALÁPAGOS COALITION

The Galápagos Coalition is an organization that works to protect the environment in the Galápagos Islands. The coalition consists of a group of biologists, scientists, and lawyers. Each of the members is an expert in a particular environmental issue. The coalition works to conserve the unique wildlife of the Galápagos and restrict the degree of human activity that takes place on the islands by both tourists and the local population.

Left: Thousands of trees are cut down to build roads in the jungle. These trees provide food and shelter for birds and animals in the forest.

conservation projects in Ecuador. Jatun Sacha runs three biological stations around the country, where the staff develop and implement programs related to forestry, environmental education, and public health. The organization is currently working on a reforestation project in Esmeraldas Province with the help of CARE-USAID foundation in the United States.

Fundación Jocotoco

The Fundación Jocotoco was established in 1998 to preserve the habitats of endangered bird species. Although the Ecuadorian government has worked very hard to preserve the most representative of the country's 1,500 bird species, many other bird species, such as the Jocotoco Antpitta, the El Oro parakeet, and the pale-headed brush-finch, among others, are dying out. Many of these birds live in areas where people cut down trees for logging or for raising cattle. The foundation buys these lands and creates reserves. In these reserves, Fundación Jocotoco implements comprehensive reforestation plans to make sure trees grow back on the cleared land. Fundación Jocotoco has established four reserves, so far. The foundation plans to create eighty more reserves in Ecuador.

Semana Santa

Nearly all Ecuadorians celebrate the Roman Catholic holiday of Semana Santa, or "Holy Week." This religious celebration is the South American equivalent of Easter and Holy Week in the United States. Semana Santa begins on Palm Sunday and lasts until Easter Sunday.

Pilgrimages

During Semana Santa, Ecuadorians take part in pilgrimages throughout the country. The final destination for pilgrimages during Semana Santa is a sacred place, usually a church. Many times, processions visit churches that house images of the Virgin Mary.

Another distinctive tradition of this religious celebration is a procession of devout Catholics who march through the streets of Ecuador carrying wooden crosses. Many of the pilgrims wear tall, cone-shaped hats and gowns open at the back. As a sign of repentance for their sins or as a sacrificial offering to God, these pilgrims sometimes carry whips, which they use to flog their backs as they march in the procession. Other pilgrims walk barefoot or do the pilgrimage on their knees.

Below: **Otavalo Indian women rest outdoors before going on a pilgrimage to celebrate Good Friday.**

The pilgrimage represents the hours before the crucifixion of Jesus Christ. One of the pilgrims acts the part of Christ and carries a cross while the other pilgrims follow behind him. Among the followers, women can be heard crying out loud, while groups of men and women sing hymns and praises.

Different plays reenacting the last days of Jesus Christ are also performed. These plays are based on famous Bible passages, such as Jesus' entry into Jerusalem on Palm Sunday, the Last Supper, and the crucifixion, and they are reenacted on the day of Holy Week that corresponds to the Biblical event. Special church services are held on Easter to celebrate the resurrection of Christ.

Above: **Pilgrims from Cotacachi hold palm leaves as they take part in a procession leading to a church on Palm Sunday.**

Special Foods

Food forms a special part of the Ecuadorian Easter celebration. Dishes consist mainly of fish due to the Catholic tradition of not eating red meat during Easter. A unique soup called *fanesca* (fah-NEHS-kah) is prepared during Semana Santa. Fanesca, a dish exclusive to Ecuador, is made with fish, rice, onions, peanuts, squash, beans, corn, lentils, peas, yucas, and potatoes.

RELATIONS WITH NORTH AMERICA

Ecuador's relations with both Canada and the United States are stable and have become closer over the past few years. All three countries belong to the Organization of American States (OAS).

Ecuador has enjoyed good relations with the United States since Ecuador's independence in the 1830s. The first U.S. consul was sent to Ecuador in 1839. Ecuador and the United States share many common concerns, such as maintaining democratic institutions, promoting free trade, protecting human rights and the environment, and fighting against the trafficking and consumption of illegal drugs. Over the years, both countries have cooperated in numerous economic and environmental programs.

Formal diplomatic relations between Ecuador and Canada started in the early 1960s. Both countries are currently working together on a number of technological and environmental projects in Ecuador, mainly targeted at the rural areas of the country.

Opposite: **The Galápagos Islands are a popular tourist destination for many North Americans, who visit the Ecuadorian islands to view rare species of plants and animals found only on the Galápagos.**

Left: **Ecuadorian president Gustavo Noboa (*middle row, far right*), Canadian prime minister Jean Chretien (*front row, far left*), and U.S. president George W. Bush (*front row, third from left*) were among North, Central, and South American leaders who attended the third Summit of the Americas in Quebec City, Canada, in April 2001.**

Foreign Relations with Canada

The first Canadian ambassador to Ecuador arrived in the country in 1961. For several years, the Canadian embassy to Ecuador operated out of Colombia, until the Canadian government set up a permanent diplomatic mission to Quito in 1989. Consular matters, however, continue to be handled by the Canadian embassy in Colombia. Ecuador set up an embassy in Ottawa, Canada, in 1972.

Ottawa Convention Banning Land Mines

Canada currently provides technical support to Ecuador, particularly in the area of information technology. Ecuador is also a subscriber to the Mine Ban Treaty, a treaty that was signed in Ottawa, Canada, in December 1997. The Canadian government, in turn, supports Ecuador's effort to deactivate and eradicate land mines, particularly along the country's southern borders.

Left: This Canadian soldier is showing his skills at defusing a land mine in front of a crowd of onlookers in Ottawa. As a firm advocate against the use of land mines, Canada has provided aid and training to Ecuador to help Ecuadorians learn how to remove or defuse the bombs.

Left: **Ecuador won the Canada Cup of Soccer in June 1999. Ecuadorian player Alberto Montano proudly holds the cup among a group of Ecuadorian fans in Edmonton, Canada.**

Canadian Connectivity

The Canadian government has recently announced Canada's intention to fund connectivity programs in Latin American countries. The purpose of these programs is to give young people living in remote areas of Latin America the chance to learn about and have access to the Internet. One of these programs has been set up in the Ecuadorian province of Esmeraldas. This program aims to improve the lives of children from poor families by providing them with informal education and computer training through the Internet.

United States Aid to Ecuador

The United States provides aid to Ecuador through a number of different government agencies and organizations. The United States Peace Corps also operates in Ecuador.

On March 30, 2000, the U.S. House of Representatives approved an allocation of U.S. $1.6 billion in emergency aid to countries in Latin America. This emergency funding is part of the Plan Colombia, which aims to assist Latin American countries in security operations to control illegal drug trade. U.S. $20 million in aid has been allocated to Ecuador through this plan.

The Overseas Private Investment Corporation (OPIC) is a U.S. government agency that provides insurance and loans to small U.S. businesses to encourage them to invest in developing markets, such as those in Latin America. The goal of OPIC is to help the economies of developing countries and create more jobs. As of 2000, OPIC has invested U.S. $94.5 million in Ecuador.

The United States has also provided aid to Ecuador through the U.S. Agency for International Development (USAID). The donations have mainly been agricultural products such as wheat, soybean oil, and soybean cakes.

Left: Ecuadorian children gathered at a theater in Quito in 1999 to attend the relaunch of the weekly television show *Arcandina*. The show was originally broadcast from 1996 to 1997 to promote awareness about environmental conservation among Ecuadorian children and teenagers. The relaunch of the program was sponsored by the Ecuadorian government and U.S. organizations, such as USAID. Here, the children are carrying a banner on which they have painted messages about protecting the environment of the Galápagos Islands.

Left: **The U.S. Coast Guard Gulf Strike Team unloads equipment to help clean up an oil spill that took place near the coast of San Cristobal Island in the Galápagos in January 2001. The United States has helped Ecuador address a number of environmental problems.**

Andean Trade Preference Act

The Andean Trade Preference Act (ATPA) is a law that was established by the United States government in December 1991. This law allows certain countries to export their merchandise duty-free to the United States. Ecuador, along with Bolivia, Colombia, and Peru, qualified for the ATPA.

The main purpose of the ATPA is to boost the economies of these countries by encouraging the export of their products to the United States. These products are not taxed, so prices are competitive in the U.S. market. Through the ATPA, the U.S. government hopes that economic conditions within these countries will also improve. The United States, in turn, benefits by importing cut flowers, fish, fish products, and other goods from Ecuador and by establishing a more effective fight against illegal drug trade.

Under the current law, the ATPA is scheduled to end in December 2001. Although the ATPA has produced significant results, the Andean countries involved have requested an extension of several more years, on the grounds that more time is needed for the law to make a significant difference in their economies. The Andean countries have also requested the addition of Venezuela as a beneficiary country.

Ecuador–Peru Peace Process

The United States has been actively involved in finding a peaceful solution to the long-standing border conflict between Ecuador and Peru. The United States was one of the guarantors of the Rio Protocol of 1942. When fighting broke out between soldiers from Ecuador and Peru in the disputed area in 1995, the United States acted as one of the mediators to bring about a cease-fire.

The United States, along with the other three guarantors of the Rio treaty, appointed a special envoy to participate in the peace negotiations between Ecuador and Peru. In addition, the guarantors agreed to hold special meetings in each country's capital city to try to find a solution to this conflict. The United States also played an active role in the Mission of Military Observers to Ecuador–Peru (MOMEP).

The United States held the second session of these scheduled meetings on February 17, 1998. Secretary of State Madeleine Albright spoke to representatives from both Ecuador and Peru during Commission II, as the meeting in the United States was named, and encouraged the cooperation of both countries to achieve peace in the disputed area. The final meeting was held in May 1998, and a peaceful solution to the conflict was finally achieved later that same year.

Left: **U.S. secretary of state Madeleine Albright signed bilateral treaties with Ecuadorian chancellor Heinz Moeller during Albright's visit to Quito in August 2000.**

Left: **Ecuadorian president Jamil Mahuad delivers a speech to the U.N. General Assembly in October 1998.**

Manta Air Base

In an effort to fight the illegal trade of drugs in South America, the United States and Ecuador signed an agreement on November 12, 1999, that allowed the U.S. military to use the Ecuadorian air base at Manta, located on Ecuador's Pacific coast. Although Ecuador is neither a producer nor a consumer of illegal drugs, the country is used as a transit area for drugs produced in other South American countries and then shipped to the United States and Europe. The ten-year agreement will allow the U.S. air force to detect any potentially illegal flights around Manta.

United Nations

In 1945, Ecuador became a member of the United Nations (U.N.) by signing the United Nations Charter. Since then, Ecuador has been an active member of the U.N. The Permanent Mission of Ecuador to the United Nations is located in New York City.

Ecuadorians in the United States

Many Ecuadorians have immigrated to the United States over the last few decades. Most of these Ecuadorians leave their homeland to seek better lives and better job opportunities. The descendants of these immigrants contribute a great deal to U.S. lifestyle and culture. Around 150,000 to 200,000 Ecuadorians currently reside in the United States, especially in New York City.

Christina Aguilera

Christina Aguilera is a well-known American artist of Ecuadorian descent. Aguilera began singing and performing at the age of six in school talent shows. One of the biggest breaks of her career came when she joined the popular T.V. program *The New Mickey Mouse Club* at the age of twelve, along with Britney Spears, J.C. and Justin of 'N Sync, and Keri Russell of *Felicity*.

Left: **Popular singer Christina Aguilera smiles as she holds a Grammy award for Best New Artist in 2000. Aguilera is an American of Ecuadorian descent.**

Above: **American actress Meg Ryan and Australian actor Russell Crowe run through an open-air market in a scene from the movie *Proof of Life*. Most of the film was shot in Ecuador.**

Aguilera's first album, titled *Christina Aguilera*, included the hit singles "What a Girl Wants" and "Genie In A Bottle." The latter song earned her a Grammy award for Best New Artist of 2000. She also won an American Latino Media Arts (ALMA) award for Best New Artist. Aguilera has expressed pride in her Ecuadorian heritage on several occasions. In 2000, Aguilera released a Spanish language album, *Mi Reflejo*.

Proof of Life

In 2000, Russell Crowe and Meg Ryan starred in *Proof of Life*, an action movie filmed in Ecuador. According to the movie's director, Taylor Hackford, Ecuador was chosen as the film's location because of the country's spectacular scenery. The director felt that of all the Latin American countries, Ecuador was best suited for the movie because the country offers views of snowcapped volcanoes as well as rain forests. The friendly Ecuadorians also made it easy for the movie crew to film in the country.

U.S. and Ecuadorian Embassies

A U.S. embassy is located in Quito, and a U.S. consulate is in Guayaquil. Thirteen Ecuadorian consulates can be found throughout the United States and Canada. The Ecuadorian Embassy to the United States is located in Washington, D.C. The role of the Ecuadorian consulates in the United States is to grant U.S. citizens traveling to Ecuador valid visas to enter the country. The consulates also keep official records of Ecuadorian citizens in the United States and Canada.

United States Information Service

The United States Information Service (USIS) is a service provided by U.S. embassies around the world. USIS provides information about American culture and society to Ecuadorians through the U.S. Embassy in Quito. The USIS is also in charge of the embassy's public affairs. USIS activities include organizing student exchange programs, giving lectures, and providing information about American society. These activities are designed to enhance foreign relations between the United States and Ecuador and to increase understanding of U.S. policies in Ecuador.

Below: **The U.S. Embassy in Quito is located on the corner of 12 de Octubre Avenue and Patria Avenue.**

Left: **An American tourist buys traditional Ecuadorian crafts from a street vendor in Quito.**

Americans in Ecuador

About fifteen thousand U.S. citizens reside in Ecuador. Most of the Americans that live in the country are businesspeople and their families. American children attend the American Spanish School in Quito, where they must take classes in English and Spanish. In addition to U.S. history, the children at the American Spanish School also learn Ecuadorian history. Many missionaries from the United States and Canada also live in Ecuador. Approximately twenty-four thousand U.S. citizens visit Ecuador every year as tourists.

Student Exchange Programs

A wide variety of student exchange programs exist between the United States, Canada, and Ecuador. One organization that places Ecuadorian students in the United States is OCEAN, or the Organization for Cultural Exchange Among Nations. Students are required to have at least a C grade point average at school in order to apply for the program.

American university students are encouraged to participate in cultural exchanges with the Universidad San Francisco. This university is located in Quito and offers an extensive foreign exchange program.

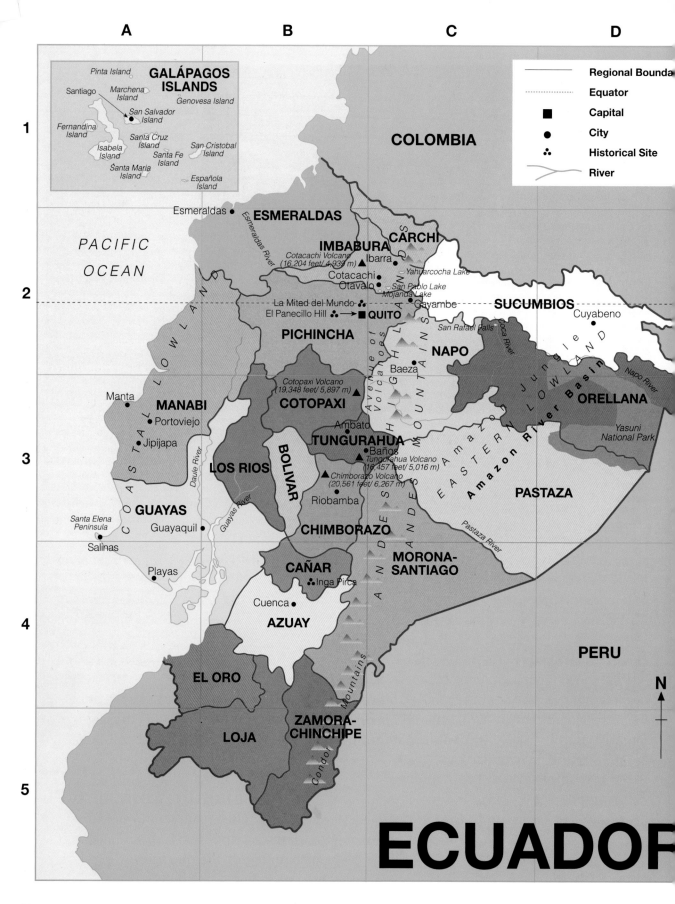

GALÁPAGOS ISLANDS

Pinta Island
Marchena Island
Santiago
San Salvador Island
Genovesa Island
Fernandina Island
Santa Cruz Island
Isabela Island
Santa Fe Island
San Cristobal Island
Santa Maria Island
Española Island

	Regional Bounda
	Equator
■	Capital
●	City
❖	Historical Site
~	River

COLOMBIA

PACIFIC OCEAN

Esmeraldas

ESMERALDAS

Esmeraldas River

CARCHI

IMBABURA

Cotacachi Volcano (16,204 feet/ 4,939 m) ▲ Ibarra

Yahuarcocha Lake

Cotacachi

Otavalo

San Pablo Lake

Mojanda Lake

La Mitad del Mundo ❖
El Panecillo Hill ❖ → ■ **QUITO**

Cayambe

SUCUMBIOS

Cuyabeno

PICHINCHA

San Rafael Falls

Oca River

NAPO

Baeza

Napo River

Cotopaxi Volcano (19,348 feet/ 5,897 m) ▲

COTOPAXI

Manta

MANABI

Portoviejo

Jipijapa

Ambato

TUNGURAHUA

Baños

Tungurahua Volcano (16,457 feet/ 5,016 m) ▲

▲ Chimborazo Volcano (20,561 feet/ 6,267 m)

Riobamba

ORELLANA

Yasuni National Park

PASTAZA

Pastaza River

Daule River

LOS RIOS

BOLIVAR

GUAYAS

Guayas River

Santa Elena Peninsula

Guayaquil

Salinas

CHIMBORAZO

CAÑAR

❖ Inga Pirca

Cuenca

MORONA-SANTIAGO

Playas

AZUAY

PERU

EL ORO

Mountains

LOJA

ZAMORA-CHINCHIPE

Condor

N

ECUADOR

 COASTAL LOWLAND

ANDES HIGHLANDS MOUNTAINS

Avenue of Volcanoes

EASTERN LOWLAND

Amazon Jungle

Amazon River Basin

Above: Modern buildings line a busy street in Guayaquil, Ecuador's largest city.

Amazon Jungle C3–D2
Amazon River Basin
 C3–D2
Ambato B3
Andes Highlands C2–C4
Andes Mountains B5–C2
Avenue of Volcanoes
 B3–C2
Azuay (province) B4

Baeza C2
Baños B3
Bolivar (province) B3

Cañar (province) B3–B4
Carchi (province) B1–C2
Cayambe C2
Chimborazo (province)
 B3–B4
Chimborazo Volcano B3
Coastal Lowland A3–B2
Coca River C2
Colombia B1–D2
Condor Mountains B4–B5
Cotacachi C2
Cotacachi Volcano B2
Cotopaxi (province)
 B2–B3
Cotopaxi Volcano B3
Cuenca B4
Cuyabeno D2

Daule River B2–B3

Eastern Lowland C3–D2
El Oro (province) A4–B4
El Panecillo Hill B2

Esmeraldas (city) B2
Esmeraldas (province)
 B1–B2
Esmeraldas River B2
Española Island A1

Fernandina Island A1

Galápagos (province) A1
Galápagos Islands A1
Genovesa Island A1
Guayaquil B3
Guayas (province) A3–B4
Guayas River B3–B4

Ibarra C2
Imbabura (province)
 B2–C2
Inga Pirca B4
Isabela Island A1

Jipijapa A3

La Mitad del Mundo B2
Loja (province) A5–B4
Los Rios (province)
 B2–B3

Manabi (province) A2–A3
Manta A3
Marchena Island A1
Mojanda Lake C2
Morona-Santiago
 (province) B4–C3

Napo (province) C2–C3
Napo River C3–D3

Orellana (province) C2–D3
Otavalo C2

Pacific Ocean A5–B1
Pastaza (province) C3–D4
Pastaza River C3–C4
Peru A4–D2
Pichincha (province)
 B2–C2
Pinta Island A1
Playas A4
Portoviejo A3

Quito B2

Riobamba B3

Salinas (beach) A3
San Cristobal Island
 A1–B1
San Pablo Lake C2

San Rafael Falls C2
San Salvador Island A1
Santa Cruz Island A1
Santa Elena Peninsula A3
Santa Fe Island A1
Santa Maria Island A1
Santiago A1
Sucumbios (province)
 C2–D2

Tungurahua (province)
 B3–C3
Tungurahua Volcano B3

Yahuarcocha Lake C2
Yasuni National Park
 D2–D3

Zamora-Chinchipe
 (province) B4–B5

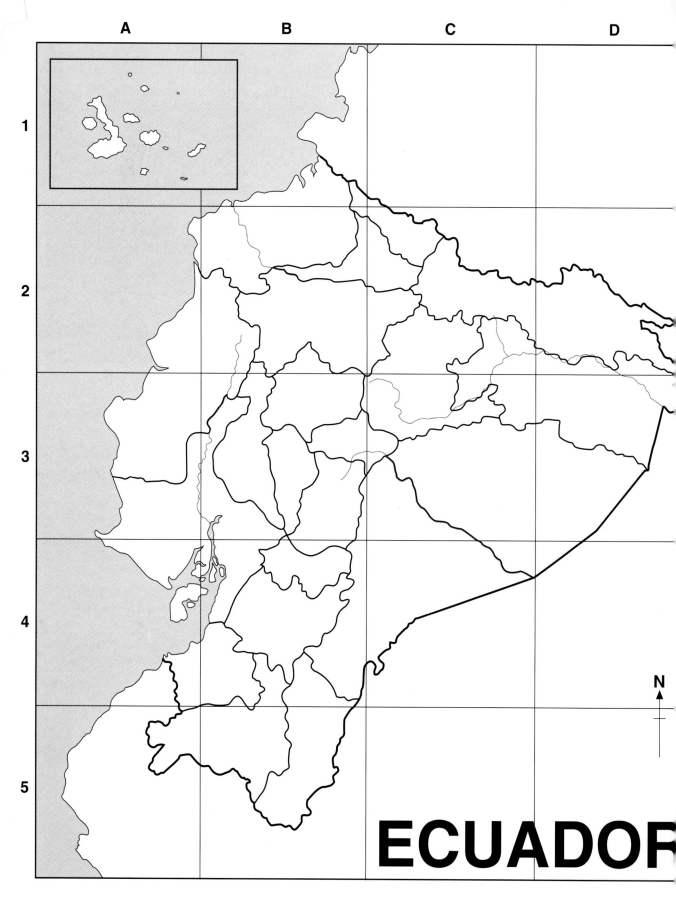

A B C D

1

2

3

4

5

N

ECUADOR

88

How Is Your Geography?

Learning to identify the main geographical areas and points of a country can be challenging. Although it may seem difficult at first to memorize the locations and spellings of major cities or the names of mountain ranges, rivers, deserts, lakes, and other prominent physical features, the end result of this effort can be very rewarding. Places you previously did not know existed will suddenly come to life when referred to in world news, whether in newspapers, television reports, or other books and reference sources. This knowledge will make you feel a bit closer to the rest of the world, with its fascinating variety of cultures and physical geography.

Used in a classroom setting, the instructor can make duplicates of this map using a copy machine. (PLEASE DO NOT WRITE IN THIS BOOK!) Students can then fill in any requested information on their individual map copies. Used one-on-one, the student can also make copies of the map on a copy machine and use them as a study tool. The student can practice identifying place names and geographical features on his or her own.

Above: **The elaborate altar of the San Francisco Cathedral in Quito is one of Ecuador's oldest pieces of colonial art. Completed in the early 1600s, the cathedral is the largest colonial structure in Ecuador.**

Ecuador at a Glance

Official Name	República del Ecuador (Republic of Ecuador)
Capital	Quito
Official Language	Spanish
Population	12.9 million
Land Area	109,483 square miles (283,560 square km)
Provinces	Azuay, Bolivar, Cañar, Carchi, Chimborazo, Cotopaxi, El Oro, Esmeraldas, Galápagos, Guayas, Imbabura, Loja, Los Rios, Manabi, Morona-Santiago, Napo, Orellana, Pastaza, Pichincha, Sucumbios, Tungurahua, Zamora-Chinchipe
Major Cities	Quito, Guayaquil, Cuenca
Highest Point	Chimborazo Volcano 20,561 feet (6,267 m)
Major Rivers	Daule, Guayas, Napo, Pastaza
Major Mountains	Chimborazo Volcano, Cotopaxi Volcano, Tungurahua Volcano
Main Religion	Roman Catholicism (95 percent)
Current President	Gustavo Noboa (from January 2000 to January 2003)
National Anthem	*Salve, O Patria* ("Hail, O Fatherland")
Important Holidays	New Year's Day (January 1)
	Carnaval (February)
	Semana Santa (March/April)
	National Day (August 10)
	Independence of Guayaquil (October 9)
	All Saints Day (November 2)
	Founding of Quito (December 6)
	Christmas Day (December 25)
Major exports	Bananas, cacao, coffee, cut flowers, fish, oil, shrimp, timber
Currency	U.S. dollar

Opposite: **This monument marks the meeting between Simón Bolívar and José de San Martín in 1822.**

Glossary

Spanish Vocabulary

ají (ah-HEE): chili peppers; Ecuadorian chili sauce.

Archipiélago de Colón (ahr-chee-pee-EH-lah-goh deh koh-LONE): the Galápagos Islands.

Carnaval (kahr-nah-VAHL): carnival; a celebration common to Catholic countries. In Ecuador, it lasts for about a week before Ash Wednesday.

castellano (kahs-teh-lee-AH-noh): the Castilian dialect spoken in South America; the Spanish language.

ceviche (seh-VEE-cheh): an Ecuadorian dish made with raw fish or seafood marinated in lemon sauce and served with raw onions and chili peppers.

charangos (chah-RAHN-gohs): small Andean guitars.

colada morada (koh-LAH-dah moh-RAH-dah): an Ecuadorian sweet drink made from corn and various berries.

compadrazgo (kohm-pah-DRAHZ-goh): the Catholic tradition of godparenting.

Costa (KOHS-tah): Coastal Lowland region in Ecuador.

costeños (kohs-TEH-nee-ohs): people living on the coast.

criollos (kree-OH-yohs): people of pure Spanish descent who were born in the Spanish colonies.

cumbia (KOOM-bee-ah): a popular dance rhythm from Colombia.

currulao (koo-roo-LAH-oh): a dance party popular with Afro-Ecuadorians.

cuy (KOO-ee): baked guinea pig.

Día de los Muertos (DEE-ah deh lohs moo-EHR-tohs): All Saints Day.

ecua-volley (EH-koo-ah-BOH-lay): a game similar to volleyball but played by two teams of only three players.

El Panecillo (ehl pah-neh-SEEL-loh): "little bread loaf;" a hill in Quito upon which stands a statue of the Virgin of Quito.

empanadas (ehm-pah-NAH-dahs): crispy pastries filled with meat or cheese.

encomiendas (ehn-koh-mee-EHN-dahs): the Spanish colonial system in which Spanish settlers were given an area of land in return for paying taxes to the Spanish king and converting the Indians in the area to Christianity.

fanesca (fah-NEHS-kah): soup made with fish, grains, beans, potatoes, and peanuts.

fútbol (FOOT-bohl): soccer.

galápagos (gah-LAH-pah-gohs): the old name for the giant tortoises that live on the Galápagos Islands.

Guayaquileños (goo-ah-yah-kee-LAY-nee-ohs): people from the city of Guayaquil.

jipijapa (hee-pee-HAH-pah): a Panama hat; a town in the province of Manabi.

Jurar la Bandera (who-RAHR lah bahn-DEH-rah): the pledge of allegiance to the flag of Ecuador.

La Mitad del Mundo (lah mee-TAHD dehl MOON-doh): "half of the world;" the monument located at the site of the equator north of Quito.

marimba (mah-REEM-bah): a percussion instrument that probably originated in South Africa.

mestizos (mehs-TEE-sohs): people of mixed European and Indian descent.

Oriente (oh-ree-EHN-teh): the Eastern Lowland region of Ecuador that consists mainly of the Amazon Jungle.

pelota nacional (peh-LOH-tah nah-see-oh-NAHL): a game played by three teams of people, in which one team stands in the middle and tries to keep the ball from bouncing back and forth between the other two teams.

peninsulares (pay-neen-soo-LAH-rehs): Spanish people born in Spain.

quinceañera (keen-seh-ah-nee-EH-rah): the fifteenth-birthday celebration of an Ecuadorian girl.

Quiteños (kee-TEH-nee-ohs): people from the city of Quito.

salchi-papas (SAHL-chee-PAH-pahs): a snack of French fries and sausages cut into pieces.

sanjuanitos (sahn-who-ah-NEE-tohs): melancholic Ecuadorian dance tunes.

Semana Santa (seh-MAH-nah SAHN-tah): Holy Week and Easter.

serranos (seh-RAH-nohs): people living in the Andes Highlands.

Sierra (see-EH-rah): the geographic region in Ecuador that contains the Andes Mountains.

soroche (soh-ROH-chay): altitude sickness.

telenovelas (teh-leh-noh-VEH-lahs): Latin American soap operas.

yuca (YOO-kah): an Andean vegetable similar to the potato.

English Vocabulary

advocate: supporter.

archaeologists: scientists who study ancient artifacts.

astute: clever, shrewd.

conquistador: a Spanish conqueror of the Americas in the sixteenth century.

demarcate: designate a boundary.

endemic: a plant or animal native to a certain region or country.

escalate: increase in intensity.

evolution: the process of changing shape or developing gradually over a long period of time in order to adapt to a changing physical environment.

heresy: religious opinion that rejects the beliefs and customs of an established church.

indigenous: originating in or characteristic of a particular region or country.

inflation: the economic condition characterized by a rise in the price of goods.

penal: relating to punishment for a crime.

peonage: a Spanish colonial system that forced the native population to work for Spanish settlers permanently in exchange for paying off debts that were assigned to them by the Spanish.

recession: a period of economic decline characterized by unemployment and a decrease in production and wages.

rhetoric: the art of effective and skillful public speaking.

solstice: one of two times in the year when the Sun is at its greatest distance from the equator. The summer solstice takes place on June 21, and the winter solstice takes place on December 22.

More Books to Read

The Ancient Incas: Chronicles from National Geographic. Cultural and Geographical Exploration series. Arthur Meier Schlesinger, ed.; Fred L. Israel, ed.; and Hiram Bingham (Chelsea House)

Children of the Ecuadorean Highlands. World's Children series. Barbara Beirne (Carolrhoda Books)

Ecuador. Cultures of the World series. Erin L. Foley (Benchmark Books)

Ecuador. Enchantment of the World series. Marion Morrison (Children's Press)

Ecuador. Major World Nations series. Sarita Kendall (Chelsea House)

Ecuador and the Galapagos Islands: The Ecotravellers' Wildlife Guide. David L. Pearson and Les Beletsky (Academic Press)

Ecuador: A Guide to the People, Politics, and Culture. In Focus series. Wilma Roos and Omer Van Renterghem (Interlink Publishing Group)

Ecuador Peru Bolivia. Country Fact Files series. Edward Parker (Raintree/Steck Vaughn)

Lost Treasure of the Inca. Peter Lourie (Boyds Mills Press)

Videos

Going Places — Volcanoes & Rainforests. (MPI Home Video)

Lonely Planet — Ecuador and the Galapagos Islands. (Lonely Planet)

National Geographic's Galápagos Islands — Land of Dragons. (National Geographic)

Web Sites

www.ecuador.com

www.ecuador.org/geninfo.html

www.ecuadorexplorer.com/html/history.html

www.jatunsacha.org/english/stations.html

Due to the dynamic nature of the Internet, some web sites stay current longer than others. To find additional web sites, use a reliable search engine with one or more of the following keywords to help you locate information on Ecuador. Keywords: *Amazon, Andes, Cuenca, equator, Galápagos, Guayaquil, Panama hats, Quito, José de Sucre.*

Index